I BELIEVE

I BELIEVE

George Carey

First published in Great Britain 1991
SPCK
Holy Trinity Church
Marylebone Road
London NW1 4DU

Acknowledgements

Bible quotations are taken from the *Revised Standard Version*,
copyright 1946 and 1952, second edition 1971, Division of
Christian Education, National Council of the Churches of
Christ in the USA. *The Letters of Abelard and Héloïse*, tr. Betty
Radice, Penguin (1974). R.S Thomas, *Later Poems 1972-1982*,
Macmillan (1983). T.S.Eliot from 'East Coker' in *Collected
Poems 1901-1962* Faber (1963).

British Library Cataloguing in Publication Data

Carey, George Leonard, b.1935
  I Believe.
  1. Sermons
  I. Title
  252

  ISBN 0-281-04532-1

Layout/typesetting: AD Publishing Services Ltd
Printed by Biddles Ltd, Guildford and King's Lynn

CONTENTS

PREFACE

It was, of course, inevitable that as news spread of my nomination to succeed Dr Robert Runcie as Archbishop of Canterbury, questions would arise concerning me. 'What is he like? Is he liberal? Conservative? Evangelical? Catholic? What does he believe and stand for?' SPCK suggested that a collection of addresses would go a long way towards answering some of these questions and would also provide a profile of what I am like as a person.

I was delighted to agree to their proposal but it is important to draw the reader's attention to the fact that what this volume consists of is a collection of unselfconscious talks, lectures and addresses given to a variety of groups over recent years. I mean by the word 'unselfconscious' that they were never intended to be presented in book form. I delivered them to audiences—often with passion and sometimes with just a few notes before me. But they were always imparted with total commitment to the task of engaging with those listening.

Readers will quickly detect certain things about my approach and style. They will notice my unashamed use of anecdote and illustration. I plead guilty to this element; indeed, I believe wholeheartedly in the importance of 'story' as a way of connecting with people. Then I hope they will see how difficult it is to put me in a theological box. I am unapologetically eclectic because I owe so much to all Christian traditions. And I do not believe I have stopped travelling theologically although I am convinced of the truth of the Christian faith and of the need to proclaim it as well as we can. Indeed, it is my hope that this volume will be seen as a small contribution to the Decade of Evangelism as themes of gospel, evangelism and church growth appear quite frequently in it.

Last of all, I am very grateful to SPCK and AD Publishing Services for their help in turning my material around so quickly and for their help in deciphering my notes and often quite atrocious writing. What mistakes remain, I must take responsibility for.

1

The Splendour of God

To Bath and Wells Diocesan Synod, 15 October 1988

What is the essential fact of our faith? I call it simply *the splendour of God*. St Paul knew all about this, of course, and that is why he was such a marvellous theologian, teacher and pastor. Listen to his language. 'Blessed be the God and Father of our Lord Jesus Christ,' (Ephesians 1.3). So begins Paul's letter to the Ephesians as he praises God for all the blessings of life and salvation. His language is rich, effusive, joyful and triumphant. He rehearses all the blessings the Christian receives: the gift of God's love, the breadth of God's grace, the freedom of God's Son and the power of God's Spirit.

Paul had much to sing about and so do we. We do well to consider the splendour of God together for a few moments because we must admit our God is often too small. We get so bogged down in the detail of church administration that our God seems to shrink with us. His interests seem confined to the quota, the parish communion, elections to Synod and so on. All these things are good and worthy, but on their own not big things. Paul's vision exhorts us to share a vision of God who is transcendent, holy and wonderful and who will remain when heaven and earth are folded up like a cloth and discarded.

Let us dig a little deeper; what is the splendour of God really like? Is the *shekinah* seen with glossy shine like a nice Japanese car straight from the factory – unused and exciting? Is it like a pop star on a stage seen from afar glittering in all the lights? Or perhaps it is like a Turin Shroud Christ, dead but not dead, glowing with an intensity which comes to us from the tomb itself? No. I have never worked up much enthusiasm for the Turin Shroud and I am glad that research has scotched that idea because I would have had to revise my theology of Christ.

He is the splendour of God, a splendour which comes to us through the ordinary weakness of our humanity which our Lord took humbly, down into the bitterness of death – real death with no irradiating rays to convince others – and which itself is transfigured into new life. This splendour of God, says Paul, expressed so fully in Christ, transforms the world, the Church and the Christian.

Being practical people we then ask: So what? What does it mean for us as we begin our life together as a synod? I think we can make three major responses to this vision.

First, *it affects our understanding of God's Church*. As long as God lasts – and I guess that will be for a long time – his people will last. But, oh, how I long for this to penetrate our church life. If God is splendid and his majesty sung by the Church triumphant, why are we so lethargic and the Church so unenthusiastic? Surely this vision should reach down into the ordinariness of our lives, affecting our worship, our preaching and our business? Surely such an inspiration would add urgency to our praying and thanksgiving to our Eucharists? Surely, it would give hope to our anxious Parochial Church Councils as they discuss the quota, the leaning tower, the quinquennial and the Christmas bazaar? Yes, of course it should, and in many places it does. I am always excited when I visit a church where there is a sense of outreach, confidence and expectancy. At the heart of such churches I believe they have caught hold of the splendour of God and want his grace, love, Spirit and freedom to be shared by all.

Second, *it affects our understanding of God's world*. To see God's splendour is to share a large vision of God's hope for the world and his universe. Look at Ephesians 1.9-10: 'For he has made known to us in all wisdom and insight the mystery of his will, according to his purpose which he set forth in Christ as a plan for the fullness of time, to unite all things in him, things in heaven and things on earth.' Certainly here is no encouragement to have a parochial view of God! Paul's vision is enormous; he saw everything having a place in God's plan and this theological vision he shares with us. What might it mean? For a start, we must remember that God's fatherly care is over all things. Against a secular world-view which assumes that nothing lasts for ever, that all things are relative, and that all things will share the same destiny of oblivion and darkness, the Christian world-view states that God *is*, and because he is we are, and we shall endure in his love. How we need to preach that message with conviction today, because it is true and because it makes all the difference.

Third, *it affects, or should affect, the way we treat God's creation.* As Christians we should be alarmed at what we are doing to the world: the pollution and the exploitation of this small planet. Our children and their children will pick up the tab of our neglect and we wonder if they will be able to pay.

The diocese of Bath and Wells is a particularly beautiful one and, standing as we do at the heart of our communities, we must be vigilant to speak out against anything that squanders the resources given to us by God. At this moment I am thinking of the second nuclear power station at Hinckley. Without making any value judgements, I simply say that we cannot afford to ignore what is happening. It is an example of the tremendous power mankind now possesses to affect irreversibly the future of our country and planet without possessing the full spiritual power to do this in God's strength. It is because this is God's world that we care – or should care – for the poor and for those in the inner city deprived of what we enjoy in natural beauty. Well did Simone Weil write:

> The beauty of the world is Christ's tender smile for us coming through matter. He is really present in the universal beauty. The love of this beauty proceeds from God dwelling in our souls and goes out to God present in the universe. It is like a sacrament.

This is the splendour of God in the world and in the Church. In this sacrament of our redemption we focus upon the splendour of God who loves us by giving and continuing to pour upon us the profusion of his grace. This Synod and future Synod debates will find their true context if, in our debates and discussions, we place before us the splendour of God.

Some years ago I met a film producer. After a while we began talking about horror movies. 'Do you know how we make those gruesome films with beasts that tower over us like ten-storey buildings and gigantic, slimy creatures that send us quivering under our seats? It's quite easy. All we do is to destroy the ordinary backcloth and replace it with a false one, and against this false sense of perspective an ant can look like a terrifying monster.' It is true that when the splendour and majesty of our God is forgotten our problems, our demands and tasks will appear to be nightmares that outstrip our resources. But God is, and because he is, we are, and our mission remains with all its fragility yet with all its exciting possibilities.

In this diocese we are going for growth in all ways – qualitative, quantitative and financial. We want to reach the young, challenge the middle-aged and keep the elderly. We want this diocese to share its Lord with all around. May the splendour of our God fill us with hope and gladness and let us with Paul exclaim: 'Blessed be the God and Father of our Lord Jesus Christ, who has blessed us in Christ with every spiritual blessing in the heavenly places.'

2

Why Should I Follow Christ?

Shepton Mallet, 27 September 1987

The theme of this service is *choice*.

In John 15.16 Jesus said: 'You did not choose me, but I chose you.' In a most important sense, God chooses and, by saying that, Jesus was emphasizing the sovereignty of God. We may think we choose him, but in reality God chooses us. Of course, Jesus was not denying the fact that we choose as well. We are not puppets; we make choices and sometimes they are good. At other times they are bad.

Why do we choose anything at all? Think, for a moment, about the things we choose: car, job, maybe even who we are going to spend the rest of our life with – husband or wife. Perhaps our choosing boils down to three qualities: they *attract* us, we find them *valuable*, and we find them *useful*. Making the right choice is extremely important. In Chaim Potok's book *Lights*, the hero as a young boy learns an important lesson. He is taken by his father to visit his uncle, who lives at the top of a skyscraper. 'Shall we walk or go up by lift?' asked his father. 'Let's walk,' answered the energetic boy. Twenty floors later, Gershon's father said: 'You have learned a very important lesson: choose *wisely!*'

Why did the disciples choose to become disciples of Jesus? Let's make it more personal. I am a modern disciple of Jesus. Why did I decide to follow him? Let me give my reasons:

Because I find the claims of Jesus very compelling

There have been many great religious teachers, but somehow Jesus eclipses them all. We may think of the character of his life – simplicity, holiness, strength – or the character of his teaching – bold, deep. I find when I look at his life that he confronts me with the kind of person I would like to be. One

of Shakespeare's characters says of another: 'He hath a daily
beauty in his life/That makes me ugly.' This is true of Jesus of
Nazareth. He did not write a book, yet his story has changed
the lives of millions. Why is that? It is because he died a death
that releases life. In some inexplicable way the death of Jesus
embraces mine and gives hope, meaning and life. Because of
who he is, we are; because of his death, we live. His resurrection still challenges and evokes belief. This is the cornerstone
of the Christian faith, and millions have been convinced of the
fact that Jesus was raised by the Father.

About thirty-three years ago, I became a Christian as a
young man. I had no church background, but I started to
explore the claims of the Christian faith and, like C.S. Lewis,
I was 'surprised by joy'. It was true, and I have no regrets. It
was a choice well made.

Because I find I need someone to follow

The human heart is a mysterious thing. You think of the
average human being and on the whole we are thinking about
decent, good, helpful human beings. At a deeper level, however, we are aware of our fragility and weakness. When I was
a prison chaplain in Durham I used to look at the youngsters
who were lined up before me and marvel at their ordinariness
– they were so like my own teenage sons and daughters!

Let me give you two quotations which go to the crux of the
problem. Jeremiah 17.9: 'The heart is deceitful above all
things, and desperately corrupt.' Desperately corrupt – that is,
it is capable of great acts of wickedness and depravity. True,
isn't it? I remember speaking to a man once who was candid
enough to say: 'You know, I feel in me at times two impulses.
On the one hand there is the capability to do very evil acts and
on the other hand I know I am capable of acts of gentleness,
mercy and love.' Pascal was quite right to define humanity as
'half devil, half angel'.

The other quotation comes from St Augustine who wrote:
'Our hearts are restless until they rest in thee.' That is, there
is a God-shaped blank in the lives of us all – we need God. I
find that Augustine's analysis goes to the centre of the human
problem. I am often concerned when I think of Western civilization. We are in the pursuit of happiness. We only see it as
including materialism: a better standard of living, more

clothes, a new hi-fi, more, more, more. This has sharpened individualism – we are only concerned for ourselves – and it has increased our greed. We shall go on wanting more and more until we realize that the true longing of the human heart is really after God. 'Our hearts are restless until they rest in thee.' Jesus invites us to choose his way of living, his way of behaving, his way of serving, his way of dying. 'Come with me', he invites.

Because I find in him an ever present Saviour and Lord
The Christian message we are celebrating is a thrilling one: that Jesus Christ is not dead but lives today. When I was young, I learned a chorus which goes:

> He lives, he lives, Christ Jesus lives today.
> He walks with me, and talks with me along life's
> narrow way.
> He lives, he lives, salvation to impart.
> You ask me how I know he lives?
> He lives within my heart.

The testimony of all of us who have found the living Christ is that he lives within us, changing us, shaping us. In the 1960s, during that foolish 'God is dead' business, one Canadian church put on its board: 'Our God isn't dead – sorry about yours!'

We Christians have, however, an apology to make. Sometimes 'churchianity' obscures 'Christianity'. Sometimes the Church gets in the way with its pomp and dull worship. We have to say 'sorry' because we have failed to express the wonderful good news of the Christian faith. We have failed to be the kind of disciples that Jesus desires, and, because of that, people do not choose to join us. Sometimes, however, when I hear people make the excuse: 'I don't go to church because there are too many hypocrites there', I long to answer: 'Don't let that bother you, one more won't make much difference!' The point is a serious one. We who follow Jesus Christ are not claiming that we are perfect, or that we know it all. What we are claiming is that we have met Someone who is worth following, who makes sense of this funny existence, who is changing our lives and who gives us something to live for.

What about you and me? I became a Christian thirty-three years ago and I have no regrets. It was the best choice I have ever made. It has not been easy, nonetheless; and no one will ever claim it is, because Christ did not say, 'Come lie on my cushion', but he said, 'Take up your cross and follow me.'

Will you choose to follow him? To accept his yoke on your life? Will you accept his discipline and love? As we come to the end of this Celebration we are all being invited to face again the challenge of the One who says in John 14.6: 'I am the way, and the truth, and the life.' The choice is ours to follow him, or to walk away from him.

3

What Must I Do to Inherit Eternal Life?

To the Diocesan 'Spirit of Youth' Weekend,
Wells Cathedral, 15 September 1990

Let us look at a familiar Bible passage from Mark 10, which is of the young man who came running to Jesus with a question: 'What must I do to inherit eternal life?' (Mark 10.17). Somehow that fellow must have heard about Jesus, seen him in action and was keen to follow. Maybe you as young people over recent years have felt the attraction of Jesus Christ and wished to follow him. Why, we might ask, would any young person come running to Jesus Christ anyway with such questions as: 'If I follow you, can I really trust you? Is your cause worthwhile? If I surrender my life to you can I trust you for it? Might I regret it in forty years' time?'

Putting it frankly, why should any modern youngster come running to Jesus at all? First of all, I can only reply simply that Jesus' life was quite unique. Nobody before or since has had such influence for so long on so many people all over the world leading to such radical transformation. I'm so glad that when I was seventeen and a half, with little knowledge of the Church, I found my way to Christ with my questions. My journey with him started then.

Second, Jesus' teaching was and is supreme – 'the greatest ethical code the world has ever seen' said Philip Nowell-Smith, a famous philosopher.

Then again, we are aware that Jesus was a man of extraordinary abilities. His contemporaries were amazed and in awe of what he was capable of.

Finally, his death and resurrection created the Church which bears his name, and is the reason why this majestic cathedral is here at Wells and why we are here worshipping this morning. No wonder the young man came running – it is the spirit of youth to come with enthusiasm, eager to get cracking.

If you are uncertain about the person of Jesus Christ and not sure about following him, then carry on thinking about him and what he offers. Read about him and make up your mind in the light of the facts. Don't be like the sign I saw in a Jerusalem window: 'I've made up my mind, don't confuse me with facts.' The facts are that Jesus Christ is impressive and still worth following today.

So if the first question is: 'Can I trust this person, Jesus?', there is a second: 'How much will it cost?' and it is the question anybody will ask if they are buying anything. Having just returned from Israel with a diocesan party, I can tell you we got used to haggling over things we wanted to buy. We could usually get the price down to half. Now in this passage of the Bible, after the young man approached Jesus, Jesus himself threw a spanner in the works. The young man did not say: 'I'll follow you on condition that I can stay in bed till 8.00', and so on. It was Jesus who made the unconditional demands: 'You must let go of your riches, your fortune, your family, your lifestyle – everything – and then come and follow me!'

Why did he say that? My guess is that the young man, in spite of all his enthusiasm and all his zeal, loved his lifestyle more than anything else and he would have made a half-hearted disciple. Jesus Christ did not and does not want anybody to play at being a Christian. Perhaps the young man really enjoyed dashing all over the desert on his 3.5 super-charged, 2-carb. camel, but there was the danger of all that getting in the way. 'Come,' Christ said, 'and let all that be second best. Are you prepared to give it all up and choose my way?'

I am convinced that the reason why most people do not follow our Lord is not because they cannot believe the Christian faith, but because they are not prepared to let go of other things. They still think that Christianity is about 'thou shalt not'. What a wrong idea! The Christ I follow never spoils life, fun and laughter. He always enriches life with his fullness, fragrance and presence.

Now what are the implications for us as our Spirit of Youth Festival draws to an end?

The first challenge is to *grow in your discipleship as a Chris-*

tian. Keep the enthusiasm running. Always remember that God's grace and strength are available and his grace is sufficient for every moment of every day. He will never give up. A friend told me recently of seeing a printing error on a church service sheet. The hymn should have been 'Our God Reigns'. Instead the printer had innocently added an extra 's', making the hymn 'Our God Resigns'! Our God never will, but he does want us to put him first.

The second challenge is to *be a full member of Christ's family*. Go back to your churches and tell others about this weekend. Claim your place as young people in the family of God. Young people may sometimes complain that although the Church says it is for all people it does not seem to be for them. I know; and I want to encourage you to claim your rightful place. Get to know older Christians, see if occasionally you can hold your own Youth Service, or make a contribution to worship on a regular basis. But also try to learn to value older ways of expressing the faith – the liturgy, the traditional hymns and the Book of Common Prayer. What we all have to appreciate is that the Church does not belong to us and our group but to the entire family of God – young and old together. So go back to your churches and continue to learn what it means to follow. You have much to offer and, please God, you will serve him in the days ahead with joy and love.

I understand that in the outback of Australia there used to be a sign which read: 'Choose your rut carefully, you will be in it for 2,000 miles!' Well, similarly choose very carefully whom you are going to follow, because the implications are crucial.

What happened to the young man? He went away very sad because he loved his possessions more than the Christ he wanted to follow. May you and I leave this weekend determined to serve Christ not only in the 'spirit of youth' but in the power of his Spirit.

4

A Faith that can Change the World

Clifton Roman Catholic Cathedral, Bristol, 1986

You may know the story of the graffiti on the wall of the British Museum which asked: 'Is there intelligent life on Earth?' An unknown humorist had replied below: 'Yes, but I am just passing through.' The Christian claims that the 'passing through' of Jesus of Nazareth was an act which interprets the entire destiny of mankind and gives us our worth. Christianity further claims that the incarnation was God's act of salvation and that just as we need air to survive, so we need Jesus Christ for our eternal well-being.

What, then, do we know about him? Let us suppose it's all a gigantic myth and that the whole of Christianity is a monstrous charade behind which nothing of substance exists – a bit like the Hans Anderson tale of the emperor with no clothes on. What do we know?

At the end of the last century the German biblical critic Bruno Bauer argued that Jesus did not exist. Such scepticism is unnecessary and unscholarly. New Testament scholarship repudiates such a response. We know that Jesus definitely lived, that he was an itinerant preacher in Palestine, that he was noted for his healing and teaching and that he died a surprising death: surprising in the sense that it was very rare for people other than criminals to die on the cross. There is no evidence to suggest that Jesus was a bad person – indeed, on the contrary, the early tradition speaks of his goodness. What we also know is that following his death his disciples carried on his ministry by asserting that he was risen. They held this unbelievable notion stubbornly, even to death. They were convinced that he had risen from the grave, and some claimed to have seen and even touched him.

Now those are the bare bones behind our Gospel records –

everything else is interpretation. The Gospels are not history in our sense of the word, they are interpretative documents written by people whose lives were transformed by an encounter with Jesus Christ.

Humankind separates into two groups by its response to the 'good news' (gospel) of the Christian Church. There are those who accept the faith of the Christian Church and call themselves after their leader as Christians; there are those who are not convinced, and they are honestly not convinced, for a variety of reasons.

First, it may be an unwillingness to allow God to take over. The cost is too great.

Second, it may be intellectual uncertainty. Some will say: 'This is a crazy way for God to act. How do I know that God has come to me in Jesus Christ? If it is so important, couldn't he have made it a little clearer? What about the competing claims of other religions? They too say that they are the way to God. Who am I to believe?'

Sadly, a third reason stops people from becoming Christians: the existence of the Christian Church. 'They claim to be God's people, but look at them; they are no different from the rest of us. If Christianity is as life-transforming as they claim it is, surely they would be better than they are.' This reminds me of Nietzsche's sarcastic comment on the Church: 'These Christians will have to look a lot more redeemed before I start believing in their Saviour!' Furthermore, say such outsiders, church people talk about Jesus reconciling people to God – 'but look at them, divided among themselves. Who can I really believe?'

I am sure that I cannot answer all these questions here, but offer them for us all to continue to ponder over.

What do Christians believe today about Jesus of Nazareth?

First, we believe that he manifests God. The word 'incarnation' is used to express that in the life of Jesus, God has appeared. The earliest traditions make it clear that Jesus appeared to people as a rather extraordinary man. No one doubted his humanity. Mark's Gospel says that people regarded him as the son of Mary and Joseph. As the ministry of Jesus developed, however, the mystery surrounding Jesus deepened. Not only did he ask searching questions about his society and about life, but he avoided questions about himself.

He avoided the term 'Messiah' and called himself the 'Son of man'. He preached the Kingdom of God and made a name for himself as a riveting speaker. Crowds flocked to hear him.

Very significantly also, the earliest traditions we possess – and some of them are non-Christian sources – say that Jesus went around healing the sick. Things came to a head and Jesus went to a lonely cross on basically two charges: first, that he claimed to be God's Messiah and therefore he was a 'blasphemer'; second, that he threatened to overthrow the establishment and therefore he was a political agitator. The mystery deepened with the claims that he had been raised by God. We must not minimize the impact and sensation this caused at the time. It changed a few fearful disciples who had fled the scene into courageous followers; it gave birth to the fellowship which would later be called 'the Church'; it changed the whole character of the Jewish holy day – from Saturday to Sunday.

From the resurrection of Jesus, Christology arose. The first Christians applied names to Jesus that they felt fitted his dignity and the impact he made on them. The names were quite staggering: Lord, Image, Word, God, Wisdom. The earliest baptismal confession was 'Jesus is Lord'. It wasn't long before an implicit doctrine of the Trinity developed.

From this encounter with Jesus the New Testament arose. The story of the Scriptures is a remarkable one in its own right and cannot be told here, but we are all one in calling the Bible God's Word, because it takes us to Jesus, the Living Word. The Bible, as well as being the thing all Christians have in common, has been in times past a point of division. Indeed, one of our current ecumenical problems is still the relationship between Bible and Church.

Let me put before you a way of handling this problem which does not require us to choose which is prior. I like to think of the relationship between Bible and Church as though they are inseparable twins whose parent is the gospel. The good news of Jesus Christ created the Church and the good news of Jesus Christ created the New Testament which testifies to him. The Christian Church, in its present variety and form, has not always held these essential elements together in a creative tension. There has been the 'Protestant' tendency to separate Scripture from the Church so that private interpretation of the Bible has dominated. The 'Catholic' tendency has been a predilection for absolutizing the Church so that the primary authority of Scripture has been obscured. Whether these observations are correct you must judge for yourself. I only want to ram home the point that the message of Jesus Christ is inconceivable without both Bible and Church, and both have their essential place in witnessing to the truths found in Christ.

Let me now go on to comment on five key descriptions of Christ provided for us in the New Testament.

Sacrifice

I choose to start with 'sacrifice' because one cannot understand 'redemption' and 'salvation' without it. The first Christians found it reasonably easy to interpret Christ's death because they lived in a society for which sacrifice was part of the woof and warp of life. For the Jew, Yahweh had set up an elaborate penitential system of finding forgiveness. The 'sin offering', 'guilt offering', 'peace offering', etc., created a cognitive framework which made the idea of atonement compelling. The same went for the Gentiles – they too lived at a time when sacrifice was part of culture. So the New Testament words, principally in Hebrews and Paul's letters, found an instant home in the hearts of people.

How do we understand it today? When we offend our consciences we don't race off to the local parish priest to sacrifice a pigeon or a lamb. Indeed, the average parish priest would be most surprised if you raced into his office or confessional and thrust a pigeon into his hands with a muttered comment, 'I made £100 at Newmarket on Saturday and I'm rather ashamed of myself'!

'Sacrifice' has therefore become a very difficult concept for modern people. God, for us, is not a being who is pleased with sacrifices, and in this we echo the words of Amos years ago who said: 'I hate, I despise your feasts . . . Even though you offer me your burnt offerings and cereal offerings, I will not accept them . . . But let justice roll down like waters, and righteousness like an ever flowing stream, (Amos 5.21-22, 24). Yet, I submit, the idea of sacrifice is far from dead in our culture. It is still very meaningful in our literature and in our lives. For example, we gladly sacrifice time and money for our children – perhaps for benefits we will never ourselves know

about. In Gordon's book *Miracle on the River Kwai* there is a
most moving account of sacrifice made by one man for his
comrades.

Another word which worries modern people is the word
'sin'. We don't often talk about 'sin' – only religious people
seem obsessed with it. 'Why couldn't God let bygones be
bygones?' said a rather bored young man one day when he
was learning about the cross. And we can sympathize with
this. Surely God can accept us as we are. After all, we are not
very bad people. So the Pelagian in us starts to rise. This is the
human disease: Do-it-yourself Christianity. Sin is not something to get excited about.

Suppose, however, there is something intrinsically wrong
with human nature? Suppose there is a tragic tear in our
personalities which stops us reaching the heights of what God
intended for human nature? Suppose sin is not so much what
we do but what we are, with its consequent effect in stunting
our growth so that we fall far short of God's goal for his
creation? The message of Christianity is that Jesus came to
deal with the power of sin in our lives and lived and died for
us. This 'dying for us' consists of Jesus becoming so identified
with our sin, need, despair and hopelessness that his death
proclaims, 'God loves you and gives himself for you!'

Redeemer
Again, the idea of redemption is not all that common in our
society. It was better known in pre-war London, when places
such as Carey Street were the home of pawnbroker shops.
Hard-up people could get some ready cash by putting some
heirloom in 'hock' and later redeeming it when their fortunes
changed. In Paul's day the notion of being purchased was
readily appreciated against a background of slavery. In Deiss-
mann's *Light from the Ancient East* there are some moving
accounts of the manumission of slaves as they are 'redeemed'
through the achievements of others. So the idea of redemption
enriched the first Christians' understanding of Christ's salvation. If he redeemed us, that meant we should be people who
lived as redeemed people. 'Do you not know that your body
is a temple of the Holy Spirit within you?' asks Paul in
1 Corinthians 6.19-20. 'You are not your own; you were
bought with a price. So glorify God in your body.'

Justifier

Another metaphor the New Testament uses is 'justification'. The word was taken from the law courts and it is a legal metaphor meaning that a person is acquitted. Now, in most judicial systems people are justified according to their innocence. If I am guilty of a crime, appropriate punishment is deserved. It is not possible in our legal system for a friend of a guilty person to step forward and say, 'I'll take his penalty.' This, nonetheless, is the meaning of the cross.

However, we have to use this analogy with the greatest possible care. God is *not* an avenging, angry God who will only be satisfied with the death of his innocent Son. The mystery of the cross cannot be deciphered by this metaphor on its own. It serves to say something about our unworthiness. If Jesus is the one who 'justifies' us and offers us this justification *in the Church* it means that salvation is a gift which he offers to us. I don't deserve it and neither do you. The Tridentine Canons and the Articles of the Church of England are one in saying that everything flows from God's grace.

When Paul speaks of justification it is usually followed by the words 'by faith'. Upon the interpretation of these words the tragic tear in the Western Church began. I do not have time to explore this now – except to say that one of the greatest ecumenical advances has taken place in this field and it is true to say that Catholics and Protestants (especially Anglicans) are closer now in our theological understanding of this than used to be the case. At the Reformation the Reformers, reacting against the excesses of medievalism, asserted the doctrine of justifying faith and, as is so often the case when one is asserting a teaching, this element was so exaggerated that the Tridentine Fathers understood the 'Protesting Christians' to deny the value of good works. On the other side, Catholic theology, by trying to affirm the value of good deeds, love as well as faith, were interpreted to be putting Christ's achievement in second place. Well did someone once define polemics as 'the dialogue of the deaf'. At the Reformation, sadly, there was little real listening.

So I want to suggest that justification is a helpful metaphor, as long as we realize its limitations. It says to my heart and yours: 'God has forgiven you in Christ. You are accepted. You are beloved; you needn't be anxious about God's love. He who

demonstrated his love for you so strongly by entering into all
the exigencies of human life has shown his commitment to
you.'

Saviour

We have all met people who have shoved tracts under our
noses and have whispered furtively 'Are you saved?' Apparently it was the scholar B.F. Westcott in the last century who
was accosted by an unfortunate Salvation Army lassie, to
whom he said: 'Do you mean *sōzomenos, sōtheis or sesōsmenos?*'
I bet she wished she had never asked! What Westcott meant
was: 'Well, lassie, do you mean "Am I being saved?" or "Am
I saved?" (as if it is final) or "Shall I be saved?"?' And we have
to say that all three are correct and have to be held together in
tension.

Again we are back in familiar Reformation territory. The
Reformers held on tenaciously to the idea that once a person
became a Christian they were made a Christian through the
Holy Spirit. They were 'saved'. You can see the dangers of this
assurance, however. It can lead to arrogance, subjectivism and
pride. Yet there is a substantial truth in it if our trust is in God.
Then from the Catholic side came the emphasis on the Christian life as a journey: 'I am being saved.' This also is true. I am
a pilgrim. Many dangers and uncertainties lie ahead, and I
must wait to see God working out his salvation in my life and
in the Church. Then the third idea is also true: 'I shall be
saved.' Salvation looks ahead to its fulfilment.

I dare to suggest as well that we should also hold on to
Jesus' Kingdom theology. Salvation is never merely spiritual.
It has social and political overtones. That is why Christians are
wrestling, as they should, with problems of inner cities, the
poor in South America and elsewhere, apartheid in South
Africa, and so on. The Bible teaches that salvation has cosmo-
logical implications – a new heaven and a new earth.

Reconciler

Finally, and all too briefly, we have the analogy of Christ as
Reconciler. Paul and other New Testament writers saw the
work of Christ as God's final work of reconciliation. Peace was
achieved through the blood of the cross. Humankind is now

restored to God and the Church becomes the place of reconciliation.

As a metaphor, 'reconciliation' is a meaningful political picture of estranged sides becoming one. As such it is probably the only New Testament analogy which is immediately relevant to modern life. We look around us at a world deeply unreconciled. We are told that at any one time there are at least twenty wars going on around the world. Such is the need for reconciliation today. If this is the state of our world, how can the Church go with the message of reconciliation when it is in such urgent need of reconciliation itself? How dare we preach 'peace' to others when our own divisions cry 'hypocrite'? This emphasizes the need for unity today because it is integral to the Church's message and mission.

In spite of this, the message of Jesus Christ is deeply healing and reconciling. I recall a young prisoner in a Durham prison finding faith and saying to me: 'I've never been so free in all my life!'

Jesus, as Sacrifice, as Redeemer, as Justifier, as Saviour and as Reconciler: five glorious pictures of our faith; a faith that can still change the world.

5

Towards a Christian Humanism

Spurgeon's College, 6 November 1985

Christian humanism may sound like a contradiction in terms. Surely a humanist is somebody who doesn't believe in God! The first humanists, however – people like Thomas More and Erasmus – were Christian thinkers with the insights of the Renaissance behind them, who believed that it was essential for Christians to bring together the spiritual and the human, the sacred and the secular, and make them one. This is a task which is still with us today.

We are living in a fragmented society whose most serious dislocation is between the human and divine. The majority of our contemporaries believe in God but give him no real place in their lives; they pray to him yet fail to see his significance for human existence. We need to remind them and ourselves that to lose sight of the spiritual end of human destiny is to lose the point of humanity. It is one of those ironies that only with God can people be fully human, and only with the spiritual does the material make sense.

Often I wonder if it is society's fault that it has lost the sense of the spiritual and sacred. Could it be that Christians, and I mean by this church-going Christians, by over-emphasizing the divine – by concentration upon the religious – have lost something crucial about humanity? Perhaps we have given to our world a distorted sense of what a Christian humanity is all about.

A number of you are going on into Christian ministry and I want to speak particularly to you, although I hope there will be elements in what I say which might be relevant to us all. What are the elements which go towards a Christian humanism? In my opinion three things stand out: a heart inflamed, a mind informed, and a humanity integrated.

A heart inflamed

Christianity is basically a heart affair. You are here not
because you were extremely keen to get a degree but, if I may
guess, because you felt called to Christian ministry and
wanted to give your all to it. We dress it up, of course, and
give it pompous titles like 'vocation' and 'holy orders' and
'given a charge', and so on. It reduces to a simple and direct
call to follow Christ and make him known.

I have been in theological education for some years now and
believe that the spiritual side of our ministry is the most
important. Although no doubt being a Christian in a Christian
college has not been easy, and although there may have been
times of spiritual barrenness and dryness, I hope you can look
back on your ministerial training as a time of real spiritual
growth. It will not be degrees or qualifications that will win
people for our Lord or build up churches, but lives transformed and hearts convinced that God is a God who acts. In
Morris West's fine book *The Shoes of the Fisherman* there is a
passage in which the revolutionary Pope is being questioned
on the kind of priests he wants for his new Church. He replies
simply: 'Those with fire in their hearts and wings on their
feet.' Fire in their hearts – this comes from a simple yet regular
heart relationship with our Lord day by day, working out
what it is to be a disciple, accepting the call to exercise our
ministry in service to one another, but most of all to him.

In my denomination at the moment there is a lot of questioning about growth. There is also talk of dying or dead
churches, and I acknowledge they exist. What we don't hear
much about is *life*, and there are many churches which are
growing rapidly and wonderfully. What I have noticed about
churches which are alive and growing is that they are usually
led by people of vision and life. Conversely, churches which
are dying are often led by ministers who have lost their way.

A mind informed

In my study I have a cartoon of a student standing before the
cross saying: 'Lord for you I'll go anywhere, climb any moun-
tain, sacrifice my time and money.' And the last picture has
him saying: 'But I didn't think you had study in mind!' It is
easy to get cynical about academic study, especially if we are
of a practical bent and just want to get out there and on with

the job. It was said of lectures at the Gregorian University in Rome that it was 'the mysterious process by which the notes of the professor were transmitted to the notebook of the student without passing through the mind of either'. This, I know, is not the method employed at Spurgeon's, and I have no doubt that as time goes on you will thank God for a thorough approach to theology which will make you a 'workman who has no need to be ashamed, rightly handling the word of truth' (2 Timothy 2.15). I am equally sure that the tools you have sharpened and honed here will make you a better communicator of the Christian message.

I would urge you all to strive for *excellence* in your preaching and teaching. Do not allow shoddy preparation to drift into your ministries because of the pressure of other things. Indeed, I would urge every one of you going out into ministry to seek ways to continue your thinking about theological issues. Try to become a specialist in one area and work away at it. In one of his books, your founder C.H. Spurgeon tells the story of a prospective student who, deficient in scholarship and application, tried to make excuses: 'God doesn't want my cleverness,' he whined. 'No,' thundered Spurgeon, 'but he doesn't want your stupidity either.' Indeed, Spurgeon is an outstanding example of a man who read avidly and drew into his net anything that he could use for the glory of God, and we should be prepared to be as professional as he was in that regard.

A humanity integrated

If I stopped my address at this point I could easily leave you with the impression that there are two ways of working out your ministries – the way of the heart, enthusiastic and hot-blooded, and the way of the mind, cold, careful and clinical. Hence my third point is all-important in bringing them together – because a humanity integrated makes it clear that we are talking about earthing our ministries and living in the world God has given to us. An unfortunate legacy of pietism in the Christian Church is that of regarding the world we live in as a basically hostile place and that the Christian should have no truck with the ungodly and unrighteous. This, of course, sets up battle stations at once and demarcates the battlegrounds between the Church and the world. I hope that we have moved a long way from that kind of world-view which considers our society to be utterly evil and tainted with wrong. I hope that we shall be able to enter our ministries affirming the very real experiences of grace that are found in the world and the joy which can be discovered in human gifts and beauty.

I met an Anglican priest a few weeks ago who came to mind as I thought about this address. He is an excellent man in many respects: earnest, godly, keen – but, sadly, almost totally lacking in joy. He neglects his family in his desire to win souls and I fear that his humourless approach to life will one day lead to his children rejecting the very faith their father spends his whole life struggling for. I wanted to say to him: 'But the ministry is not meant to be like this! Enjoy yourself, learn to laugh at yourself; don't take yourself or your parishioners so seriously; take a day off and be a human being; enter into as much of culture as your leisure permits; enjoy your family life and don't neglect your wife. Don't sell them or yourself short.' I lacked the courage to say that to him, mainly because I do not know him well and it would have seemed a hard thing at the time. I say it to you because the Jesus Christ I follow does not take the technicolour out of life but, rather, puts it in. The trouble with ministry is that it often sets us apart, and we need to remind ourselves often that a true biblical humanism takes seriously our 'ordinariness' and our identity with our world.

So, working towards a Christian humanism, we will want to bring the heart, the mind and our humanity with all its sinfulness, weakness and longings to an integrated humanness which has God at the centre of life and which affirms gladly and wholeheartedly all joys, sadnesses and opportunities of human existence.

6

Justification by Faith and Christian Living

To East Midlands Diocesan Evangelical Fellowship,
25 January 1986

'Justification by faith' is hardly a common expression these days, even in the Church, and we can very easily misunderstand what it means.

In Galatians 2 Paul tackles the theme of the Law and explores the nature of salvation. He tells us that God's salvation is not dependent on our good acts, or obedience to any manmade or even God-given law. 'We . . . know', says Paul, 'that a man is not justified by works of the law but through faith in Jesus Christ . . . because by works of the law shall no one be justified' (Galatians 2.16). Paul is declaring that none of the things we boast about, or trust in – intellect, upbringing, orthodoxy, good life, and so on – are vehicles of salvation. Each is tarnished by sin and, clothed in these acts of righteousness, I am clothed in rags before Almighty God. Yet, says Paul, what the Law could not do, Christ did: he identified himself with my sin and took my place. So we have that remarkable verse, Galatians 3.13: 'Christ redeemed us from the curse of the law, having become a curse for us.' Here we have a wonderful insight. Christ, in some mysterious way, takes upon himself our folly and failure and makes it his own, so that we may go free. I say 'mysterious', and so it must remain.

Paul Zahl in his book *Deliver us from Evil* gives a graphic illustration of a bush fire sweeping towards two duck hunters. The roar of the crackling fire drew near and doom seemed inevitable. Then the more experienced hunter struck a match and, lighting another fire, they stood on the leeward side of the new fire. That, too, roared away. Then the pair of them returned to the place of the burnt-out patch and in the relative safety of that refuge huddled there as the bush fire swept down on them. They escaped because where fire had passed fire could not come.

It is a useful illustration as long as we remember that no illustration is exact. God's judgement is not impersonal. Nevertheless, Paul is saying that Jesus' death affected him so profoundly that by standing in his shadow he is forgiven and justified.

Paul now adds another element. Justification 'by grace through faith' means that Christ's righteousness is 'imputed' to me. 'Abraham "believed God, and it was reckoned to him as righteousness"' (Galatians 3.6). Now, how can it be that believing can be 'reckoned' as righteousness? It seems as improbable as a foodless meal! However, our error is to think of God's Law as though it were a legal system. Israel's great sin wasn't that it did not do good things – but that it did not *obey* the Law, the Torah. It wasn't committed to its God and wasn't therefore committed to his way of doing things. The point about the story of Abraham, which is a key paradigm in Galatians, is that he obeyed God and committed himself, his family and his future to God. He left home on the word of promise; he was prepared to sacrifice his son because God said so; and his trust in God was estimated in terms of relationship to God. God was saying in so many words: 'Because he trusted in me and put me first I will honour him. He is my son.' God's righteousness was, therefore, imputed to him; reckoned as if he were the most holy person of all.

Finally, justification means a new relationship has begun. We are redeemed, made new. Christ now takes possession of us. Galatians 2.20 must be among the most marvellous words of the Bible: 'I have been crucified with Christ; it is no longer I who live, but Christ who lives in me; and the life I now live in the flesh I live by faith in the Son of God, who loved me and gave himself for me.' That is, the person who is justified is now under new ownership. A new relationship has begun, with the most momentous consequences for life, and we are going to look at some of those consequences soon.

First we must pull this together. Justification by faith means that Christ's righteousness is ours; it has been imputed to us. It does not mean that we have been made righteous as if we are perfect and free from sin, because our daily experience will tell us of the power of sin; but it does mean that we are *declared* righteous. God says to us, 'Yes, you are guilty, unworthy and deserving of punishment but I have provided for your forgiveness.' That was Martin Luther's great discovery, that salvation comes from God's grace and it is made available through faith. Luther saw that it was not a matter of his own work but God's work. 'God so loved the world that he gave his only Son that whoever believes in him should not perish but have eternal life' (John 3.16). 'When I saw that the Law meant one thing and the Gospel another', said Luther, 'I broke through.'

Now this idea came under tremendous attack because the Church of Luther's day thought that he was denying good works and asserting personal experience. This doctrine of justification subsequently broke the Western Church in two. Speaking in the Week of Prayer for Christian Unity, it would be all too tempting for Protestants to say to Catholics: 'This is the doctrine which still divides, and unless you accept this doctrine too, you cannot be saved.' Let me say a few things about this.

First, there is no denying the tragedy of separated Christians, and I for one long for the Church to be one. It is a great joy to report that on this doctrine a growing convergence is coming about between Catholics and Protestants as we have begun the demanding task of doing theology together.

Second, no one is saved by a doctrine. Justification by faith does not save us. Only Christ does and can. Justification is a descriptive doctrine; it is a way of explaining what God does for us in Christ.

Third, many will point out that justification is conspicuous in the New Testament by its absence. It is essentially a Pauline concept. It is not found on the lips of Jesus, rarely in the Acts of the Apostles and never in John. Why, some might question, is there such an emphasis on something which is so peripheral to the New Testament? The answer we readily give is that it is significant because it sums up the gospel. The word 'Trinity' is not a biblical word, but no Christian will want to say that it is insignificant. It describes God to us. Justification by faith, similarly, is important only because it goes to the heart of what it is to be a follower of Christ.

We see then that the idea introduces us to a radical gospel which brings an uncomfortable message to our hearts. It says: 'You are dead in trespasses and sins, but God is on your side.

He wants you back with him. Turn to him and the gospel will declare, "You are accepted."'

A radical gospel has radical implications, however, and to these we turn.

A radical personal life
One of Luther's great statements about justification was that of our standing before God as *simul justus et peccator* – that we are sinful and yet righteous before God at the same time. It was one of those very profound observations which was misunderstood at the time but is now widely accepted by Roman Catholic scholars among others. Being 'sinful' and 'just' is not the equivalent of having your cake and eating it, but an existential awareness of what it is to be a human being in a sinful and fallen world. By grace I am saved and therefore Christ's righteousness is attributed to me. That means, Luther said, God sees me as holy in Christ. Nevertheless, as long as I am in this world I remain a sinner, still capable of letting him down. Let me give two illustrations that might unpack this a little more.

When I was a student one of my fellow students was a fairly rude, arrogant young man. One day after a very difficult time with him, I exploded and said to him: 'I can't say that the Christian faith has made much difference to your life!' To this he calmly replied, with more charity than I deserved: 'Well, you should have seen what I was like before I became one!' There is a verse from a hymn, attributed to John Newton:

> I am not what I ought to be,
> I am not what one day I hope to be,
> But, praise God, I am not what I used to be,
> And I am what I am by the grace of God.

A rather convoluted verse, but how right it is! The first radical lesson is to stop pretending: you are accepted!

The second illustration came from my parish ministry in Durham. Tony and Margaret were childless and they befriended Stephen, a boy in a Barnardo's home. Stephen was a normal boy of seven, full of life and fun and pranks. Eventually he moved into their home and they prepared to adopt him. They told him they were going to do this, the papers were

signed and he became their son. Then one day, Margaret came
to see me. They were worried. It wasn't working out as they
had hoped. Stephen was strung up about something, and was
behaving unnaturally. Margaret explained: 'Stephen seems to
be trying too hard. He is so anxious about being accepted that
he is trying to be extra good and even perfect.' Stephen's
problem, in short, was that he was not living as a son but as a
slave in bondage to fear. So after talking it over with me, Tony
and Margaret sat down with him and said: 'Stephen, look,
here are the adoption papers. You are our son, our child. We
chose you, you belong to us. We will never send you back.
However naughty you are we will still love you.' It was as if
a great load fell from his shoulders.

In many ways we Christians also need to be reminded of
our position before God. I think it was Professor Thomas
Torrance who replied to a question concerning his 'conversion' with the reply: 'I have been converted three times. First
I was saved in eternity in the plan of God the Father, next I
was saved at Calvary through the atoning work of God the
Son, finally I was saved on Monday 30 June 19— through the
converting work of God the Holy Spirit.' Here we see the work
of the Trinity in our lives. The equivalent of Stephen's adoption papers is the cross of Christ which blazons abroad 'This
is the place where your pardon was sealed'. Calvary declares
that you are 'ransomed, healed, restored, forgiven'.

The joy of knowing forgiveness

God's intention is that everyone should enjoy the birthright of
assurance. There is no escaping the note of joy in the New
Testament about the Christian life. Read Acts and you will see
it appearing again and again. It wasn't emotionalism; it was
the joy of knowing that they were forgiven people, made new
through the gift of salvation and the gift of the Spirit. James
Denney wrote:

> Nothing is more characteristic of churches than their
> attitude to assurance and the place they give to it in their
> preaching and systems of doctrine. Speaking broadly, we
> may say that in the Roman church it is regarded as pres-
> umption, in the Protestant churches it is a privilege or a
> duty, but in the New Testament it is simply a fact. This

explains the joy which side by side with the sense of infinite obligation is the characteristic note of apostolic Christianity.

In a biography about the godly E.B. Pusey, one of the Tractarians of the last century, this is written:

The absence of joy in his religious life was only the inevitable effect of his conception of God's method of saving man; in parting with the Lutheran truth concerning justification he parted with the springs of gladness.

Whether or not the biographer was right, it is true that once you can exclaim 'Abba, Father!', joy is the accompanying fruit of the Spirit and it sheds its radiance over life and death. Indeed it transforms death and gives hope where there was darkness.

A transformed emotional life
Justification by faith means that once I am accepted I can begin to live with myself.

I never cease to be amazed at the damage human beings do to one another. In my pastoral ministry I have met so many people, some of them convinced Evangelicals, who believe in justification by faith with their heads, yet are condemned by their hearts. Peter was a very successful academic with an enormous salary, a lovely family and supportive wife. Yet at the age of forty he still regarded himself a failure because his mother had projected on to him her anxieties to such an extent that he never felt he matched up to her expectation of him. He was only able to shed that bondage through a charismatic experience which reassured him that he was a child of God. I would not be surprised if today there are a number of people who, though fully Christian, have never allowed justification by faith to be an experiential reality in their life. To put it another way, they have never really allowed its truth to blossom into fullness of life. Certainly Paul's experience expressed in Galatians 2.20 is that of Christ's life and love possessing him fully.

The outworking of the Spirit in our lives

In Galatians 3.2, Paul asks: 'Did you receive the Spirit by works of the law, or by hearing with faith?' He concludes that it is by faith. Now Paul only mentions this incidentally, but it certainly corroborates the testimony of Acts to the working of the Spirit in the early Church. In Scripture the Holy Spirit works in a twofold way in our lives.

First, he is the *Spirit of holiness*. Many have scoffed at justification by faith, believing that it is a fiction only, a make-believe doctrine that has no reality in fact. But justification is never merely a doctrine. If it does not result in a changed life, a holy life, there is no reality about it – there is, in short, no justification. There is, I want to argue, a direct correlation between justification by faith and a holy life. If you are going to preach conversion – and I hope we shall in many different ways and, skilfully, with many different nuances – you cannot avoid the consequences: it is going to lead to transformed lives. A girl who became a Christian at university went back home to her sceptical parents. Before she returned to her college her father said to her: 'Well, I don't know what to make of your religion – but I will say this, it's made you easier to live with.' That is a testimony which is often heard. Christianity affects our lives. It has a practical outworking in the way we live.

Then, the second work of the Holy Spirit is *to make weak people strong*. For too long we have lived with no expectation of renewal, or growth, or power. The person who is justified, the church which believes this, Christians who believe in a God who changes lives, cannot just simply go through the motions. The faith not only has an experiential reality, it has dynamic consequences as well. So, it is not at all surprising that the church which launches out in faith will find the power of God at hand. I pray that the Church will learn to live adventurously on the frontier of faith.

A radical effect on church life

Just as we individually are *simul justus et peccator* so is the Church – holy in Christ, yet sinful in itself. Spurgeon was right to say to that lady who left his church to join a church she felt was perfect: 'Well, Madam, when you find your perfect church don't join it – you'll only spoil it!' When we get fed up with the worship, the vicar, the organist, or other elements of church life, we should remember that justification by faith in the fellowship means accepting that our differences are as important to God as our similarities. I would like to see justification by faith working its way through our fellowships, enabling us to accept one another on the basis of our fellowship in Christ. Be on the look-out when Pelagianism sets in: 'Thou shalt be justified by good works', by doing the vicar's mail, by the way you read the lessons, by the work you do towards the Christmas bazaar! Be on the look-out when ordinary people are despised because they don't speak the way you do, or because they come from the council estate. We have to ask of our church life: Do our structures and our services proclaim this doctrine of acceptance and freedom in Christ?

We have considered a topic which is, perhaps regrettably, not at the centre of Anglican attention. I don't want to get it out of proportion with other great doctrines of the faith, but this subject goes to the very heart of the gospel and has radical implications for everyday life. I want to say in conclusion that it has as many consequences for the devout Evangelical as it does for the hardened Catholic. We have to confess that Evangelicalism has sometimes, perhaps even often, expressed itself in a hard, legalistic framework leading to a dull and often joyless form of Christianity. This ought not to be the case. Justification is, as I have said, a declarative doctrine that we are sons and daughters of a heavenly Father. As Paul says in Romans 8.15-17: 'When we cry, "Abba! Father!" it is the Spirit himself bearing witness with our spirit that we are children of God, and if children, then heirs.' What a wonderful truth! Isn't it about time we started living off our inheritance?

7

Fundamentalism – Friend or Foe?

York Minster, 1 May 1987

It may seem rather surprising to some that the Principal of Trinity College should be giving a lecture on fundamentalism and subjecting it to some criticism. After all, did not a distinguished predecessor of mine write an important book in the 1950s entitled *Fundamentalism and the Word of God*? I ought to explain that in this talk I am not attacking fundamentalism as such – I am in fact asking what are its strengths, weaknesses and challenges. Perhaps most importantly of all, I am asking what Anglicanism can learn from this trend in church life.

What *is* fundamentalism? I need not tell you how topical this subject is. Perhaps you saw the two TV programmes on American fundamentalism recently which put the ghastly and unacceptable face of that form of fundamentalism before us. It is a fundamentalism which imposes an edifice of avarice, deception and patriotism on the claims of Jesus Christ. We must remember, of course, that many fundamentalists wholeheartedly reject that type of Christian behaviour. It is not typical of fundamentalism.

Fundamentalism at its simplest is the reduction of a faith, a political creed or a way of life to an extreme and recognizable core which dominates that faith. This core is elevated to the position of an absolute which is inviolable, sacred and undisputed – undisputed, that is, by the faithful. No criticism is allowed to touch this Mount Olympus of belief; unquestioning faith and obedience is required to keep the believer within the fold of the faith. This kind of fundamentalism is easily identifiable in the world today. We see it in the fundamentalism of Shiite Islam, where blind faith sends thousands of people to a pointless war. We may see it even in political fundamentalism – where the teachings of a reformer are still seen as the crystal clear teachings which are the pure source of revelation, and from which deviation is heresy.

There is, of course, the fundamentalism of tradition. When certain assumptions are challenged, such as the ordination of women to the priesthood, suddenly tradition is seen as an inviolable and fixed form of living truth which compels the Church for ever to say 'no' to the ordination of women. When the Alternative Service Book was threatening the absolutism of the Book of Common Prayer a few years ago, the Book of Common Prayer was being spoken of as if it were on a par with Holy Writ. The story goes that when the House of Commons was discussing this issue, a leading politician was heard to exclaim: 'If the Book of Common Prayer was good enough for St Paul, it is good enough for me!'

Fundamentalism, then, is a simple expression of a faith which is said to enshrine the sacred tenets of a belief-structure. It resists criticism and usually stands over against the culture of its day.

Let me now go on from this point to comment on the so-called death of biblical fundamentalism. The story of biblical criticism has been so well documented and so often told that I will not recount it. Suffice it to say that after two centuries of higher and lower criticism we just cannot approach the Bible in the way that former Christians did. This conclusion, I want to argue, does not lead to a rejection of the Bible or to a diminution of its claims or, necessarily, to a weakening of its authority. I have found criticism to be a deeply enriching, but not always comfortable exploration of the text of Scripture.

Let me share with you two illustrations. First, I recall that when I was a theological student, having come from a fairly conservative church, I could not square up 1 Kings with 1 Chronicles. They cover the same period of history and yet talk about it in completely different ways. It seemed to me at the time that this fact did not square with claims that the Bible was inerrant. I went to see a leading Evangelical Bible teacher. He listened to my question and said: 'The difference is easily explained: imagine Kings to be a photograph and Chronicles to be a portrait – both are true.' He thought that this solved the problem, but it did not – it was a silly, thoughtless and trivial glossing over of the essential differences in the text.

These differences are better explained not by that kind of analogy, but by a recognition of the complex history of the text within the history of an ancient tribe – a history that is sometimes romanticized, sometimes idealized, and in which past and present are sometimes confusingly mixed.

Let me develop that with my second illustration. In 2 Samuel 24 the account is given of God prompting David to hold a census. David is consequently punished for this action. David is compelled to choose between three classical punishments – disasters, famine or pestilence. He chooses the latter. While the pestilence is raging, he buys the threshing floor of Araunah for 50 shekels, an altar is built and, after he has made a sacrifice, the pestilence ceases. If we look, however, at 1 Chronicles 21 where the same story occurs, we will notice some remarkable differences. It is not God, but Satan who prompts David to his perverse deed. David, at the end of the story, does not buy the threshing floor, but gives the owner 600 shekels. The sacrifice is not consumed by the fire David has built, but by lightning from heaven.

Now, how does one handle that kind of difference? You can, of course, say the stories are not identical – and this is the device of fundamentalist theologians. To my mind, however, the stories are clearly the same. The only realistic interpretation is to recognize that the differences are theological. For the writer of 1 Samuel, the story is to explain why the temple was built on the threshing floor of Araunah. David bought the place and his sacrifice was well pleasing to God. For the writer of Chronicles, it is now impossible for this later Jewish community to say that God sent this punishment – it must have been the devil. God nonetheless confirms the choice for the temple by the lightning.

This, I think, is a clear example of the way Bible writers filled out the past quite boldly, introducing modifications from their own time. Now I acknowledge that this kind of exegesis might be disturbing for some, but I believe that it is important for us as modern Christians to feel the force of this criticism which has thrown fresh light on the Scriptures as we have received them.

Fundamentalism, however, refuses to hear this sort of criticism. It has already made up its mind what kind of literature the Bible is. Its conclusion is that there are no mistakes whatever in it, and, if any apparent mistakes are found, this must be due to our interpretation and not to problems in the text. After all, what the Bible says, *God* says. Perhaps that last phrase gives us a clue as to why fundamentalism holds on so tenaciously to life. It is in essence a theological position which has already decided in advance that the Bible is the pure undistilled fountain of God's clear revelation and that to doubt its veracity in just one particular is to bring the entire edifice to the ground. The point I am making is that, from the viewpoint of scholarship, fundamentalism is dead, but it won't lie down at the grass roots level. We still find Christian undergraduates entering universities, and ordinands coming into theological colleges, who have no idea of the tremendous advances that have been made in biblical scholarship and whose first contact with historical criticism is a dismaying and frightening experience instead of, as I think it ought to be, a liberating and wholly enhancing experience.

In the Christian Church, fundamentalism sweeps on. We see the resurgence in the new nonconformism of the house churches and sometimes in the charismatic movement. It often appears in General Synod with some unspoken assumptions about the text of the Bible. For example, without wishing to go into the debate about the Bishop of Durham's well-known views – and I want to say here that on the resurrection and virgin birth I take the traditional teaching of the Church – I am concerned when speakers are ignorant of some of the critical insights which have given rise to the Bishop's well thought-out views. David Jenkins, on both issues, is giving expression to conclusions widely held by some contemporary New Testament scholars. By simply shouting him down, the issues will not go away; they have to be faced maturely and rationally, within the context, of course, of faith.

Why, I ask again, do we hear the strident voices of fundamentalism? Clearly it is a searching for *security*. We live in a world of uncertainty, where the politicians, church leaders and others have failed. 'Let us return again', they cry, 'to the source of the faith' – to the purity of Shiite Islam, to a Bible which is safe and secure or to the creed which made our nation great. The 'Moral Majority' in the United States is precisely that kind of quest for security. The moral decline of the West cries out for a return to the morals of Protestant Christianity which will tell the nation what they must do to be strong once more. We want to know what to believe, what to do, how to live the godly life.

As well as being a cry for security, however, it is also an assumption that *liberalism has failed*. I shall be elaborating upon this point in a short while, but for the moment let us observe that fundamentalism has flowered because it has concluded that liberalism is effete, ineffectual and impoverished. A return to scriptural authority is the only answer.

Putting these answers together we can see that at the heart of fundamentalism is a longing for a faith which is secure, tangible, successful, simple. Indeed, one of the strengths of fundamentalism is that its apologetics are within the reach of the average man and woman. It offers an apparently rational faith which is plausible and coherent.

Let us look now at some problems of this neo-fundamentalism as I have observed them in modern church life.

First, *it has an irrational and anti-intellectual basis*. The fundamentalist is afraid to live with questions. The intellectual exploration of the Christian faith, the careful critical examination of the Bible (however reverently the task is carried out) is not for the 'true' Bible student. Thus, the only way to understand Scripture is to submit to what it is saying at face value. This means, of course, that the kind of contradiction I mentioned earlier is rarely discovered by the average fundamentalist because their one-dimensional way of tackling the text, a few verses at a time, will not lead them to make these uncomfortable and, I think, liberating discoveries. They will not be led by preachers at their church to face up to the fact that there are four Gospels, that John is significantly different from the Synoptics, that the New Testament writers do not always speak with the same voice even on essential matters of faith.

Second, *fundamentalism is a ghetto-like escape from the world*. I heard a few weeks ago of the formation of an American group called 'Fundamentalists Anonymous'. It is an equivalent of Alcoholics Anonymous, that is, those who were trying to escape from frightening fundamentalism which had destroyed their lives. One girl shared her story of a fringe group, which for ten years had dominated her life. It had told her what to believe, how to live. She had to submit the control of her ambitions, career and money to a group over her who 'shepherded' her. What led her to make the break? She replied, simply: 'One day reading the Bible I was struck by the simple and loving demands of Jesus on his disciples and the intolerable demands of those who claimed to be Christ for me. Perhaps over a period of months, even years, the yearning grew to escape. One day I walked out of the house, leaving all my possessions. I cannot go back, I know they would reclaim me.' Groups like that have tremendous power in the United States but they are marginalized on the culture of America, having formidable influence but not respected or trusted. As a ghetto they create their own lifestyles and moral values and often express theologies that are anti-Christian as well as anti-human – Pelagian, Arminian and gnostic.

Third, *fundamentalist structures can be demonic in their influence and power.* I have already spoken of the term 'shepherding', which is well known in house churches, even in our own country. I am sure that in the majority of instances the shepherding done by leaders is done very responsibly, but this need not be the case. You see, the structure of authority is often set up to consolidate the position of the leader. The Bible, they claim, is authoritative. It is our only inspired authority, but it is interpreted through our leadership. No pope in history has ever had as much power over the lives of his flock as some of these self-styled leaders in the Western fellowships. Again, the two TV programmes I mentioned give plenty of evidence of the power they exercise over the lives of thousands upon thousands.

What is the challenge of fundamentalism? This is my real concern. It is a challenge as well as a threat. Some of you may have read James Barr's books on fundamentalism. They do not reach the true fundamentalist, because even if he read them, he would be left quite unmoved because James Barr's theology does not give a viable and positive alternative to fundamentalism.

Let me present some of the challenges to us.

The challenge of enthusiasm. Fundamentalists believe in the reality of their message and of the Jesus they preach. They give time and money to their faith and such giving often shames those of us who claim to be orthodox believers.

The challenge of expectancy. Fundamentalists believe so

totally in the reality of their message and of the Jesus they preach that they expect lives to be touched and changed. They expect and they grow.

The challenge of simplicity. Fundamentalists believe so confidently in the reality of their message and of the Jesus they preach that it is within the reach of the average person.

Of course, as I have already remarked, there is much that is wrong with their approach. Their very simplicity contains the seeds of its own weakness, because once the intelligent fundamentalist begins to enter into a true dialogue with his faith, he is remorselessly swept away from the simple truths which once satisfied him.

So what is the task of the Church in refuting fundamentalism? The essence of Anglicanism is that the basis of our authority is located within the nexus of three sources – Bible, Church and reason. The Bible is for us the primary source of authority but not the only source. Here is the heart of Anglican comprehensiveness – this is why Evangelical, Catholic and liberal can all claim to have equal shares in the treasures of Anglicanism. I think, therefore, that as Anglicans we ought to be affirming more confidently than we usually do the freedom this gives to the mind, the heart and the body to be an integrated whole. Firmness of faith and tolerance of expression is a genuine virtue to offer the Christian. Others do not often see this as a genuine option, however, so how may we present a more positive image?

We should, I think, show the reality of a godly, reflective yet positively critical approach to the Bible. We cannot deny the reality of biblical scholarship and this has to be expressed clearly. Karl Barth once said that 'the best apologetic is a good dogmatic'. He meant by this that people are more likely to be convinced of the reality of the faith if our expression of it is coherent, sensible and entire. I long for Anglican churches to be more confident in their expression of the Good News. Instead, we squander our unique position in society and nation by often giving the impression that it does not matter what we believe or how we behave. It is little wonder that fundamentalist sects have a field day welcoming in disillusioned people who have been put off Christianity by forms of Anglicanism which offer so little and demand nothing.

Now, it is important to say that an intelligent expression of faith will still convey some sense of uncertainty. That is inevitable and – I repeat – exciting and disturbing. It is inevitable because we cannot deny what we discover in Scripture. Let me give a few illustrations.

First, *homosexuality*. It is easy to go to the odd verse or two in the Bible and conclude triumphantly that homosexuality is a great evil and homosexual practices can never be condoned. That argument, by the way, I am not rejecting; it is a perfectly valid response. The careful exegete, however, will also be troubled by the fact that the Bible hardly majors on this issue, that we do not know the context of Paul's two references to the subject, and that a strong anti-homosexual line is only possible if one has already assumed that such statements are immediately transferable into our situation straight from the biblical period.

Second, *divorce and remarriage*. The New Testament is hardly unequivocal on this matter. Mark, the earliest Gospel, makes it sound as if Jesus does not allow divorce under any circumstance; but Matthew modifies it to allow that some circumstances may make remarriage legitimate. Paul in 1 Corinthians 7 seems to put another slant on this from the perspective of Roman life in the first century.

Third, *ordination of women and the issue of headship*. Paul seems to teach clearly that women should keep silent in church, and should not have authority over men in any shape or form. When we approach the text, however, the problems mount and the issues become more complicated. For example, headship is usually used in the context of marriage. How does this affect ministry? When Paul (or the writer) in 1 Timothy 2 talks about women not teaching men he makes this an absolute because he was reflecting Jewish society at the time. To follow the logic of his thought would mean banning any form of contact between men and women where women have authority over men.

A more fundamental question is: to what extent do we allow cultural elements of the first century to be transferred to our day? Such things may be seen by some as the inevitable watering down of the faith; that the alternative to fundamentalism is a blurring of the lines and the inability of the Church to address the world. On the contrary! I want to submit that it means that we do not go to the world with a watertight

message which demands 'take it or leave it'. Rather we go with
a gospel of love which invites others to meet a Lord who is
merciful, compassionate, and whose yoke is easy.

A friend of mine met up with a keen Christian woman
whose life was a mess. Her marriage was on the rocks, she had
had a breakdown, her social life was in ruins and yet when she
came to ask for his help she was wearing a sweatshirt which
had the slogan on it, 'Christ is the answer'. He took one look
at it and said to her, 'Jean, I think you should scrap the idea
that Christ is the answer. He never said that. He said, "I am
the way". I think that with him you must seek the answer to
your problem.'

That man put his finger on something very important. The
Christian life is not a tidy, ready-made road which leads
directly, simply and painlessly to the gates of heaven. Sometimes the road seems to go away from it, sometimes we cannot
see where it is going, even if there is a purpose to it. Sometimes, perhaps often, on that road we have many encourage-
ments; there come signs of God's grace. Yet it is all so
provisional and incomplete. On the other hand, as we travel
on we find that the road does appear to be leading somewhere.
We find it a hard, yet meaningful road to travel because it fits
in with our experience of life – the disappointments as well as
the joys. Such an open faith, I believe, has much to commend
it. It holds together in tension the reality of Christ in his
Church, but the Christ who is real is not only risen but is
crucified as well. The Church and the Christian live both sides
of the resurrection, and woe betide us if we forget that fact.

Fundamentalism – friend or foe? As you will have picked up,
in my opinion fundamentalism is a dangerous enemy which
has to be attacked at the level of the mind and of the heart. It
is comparatively easy to put it down intellectually. It is much
more difficult to show that it is a spiritual dead-end which will
only end in disappointment, superficiality and naivety. We
must combat it with the weapons of faith by showing that it
is possible to have a balanced, intelligent faith which offers
hope and healing. The Anglican Church is being challenged
today to put its own house in order, to show that its portrayal
of truth need not end in a sterile liberalism or empty liturgical
forms, but in a faith 'Catholic and Reformed' which, to mis-

quote Gregory the Great slightly, is 'a faith large enough for elephants to swim in and little lambs to paddle with safety'.

8

Is God Green?
To the Green Party, Wells Town Hall, 20 March 1990

I must begin by rejecting a notion that is circulating at the moment that Christianity has only recently discovered the importance of green issues and has simply jumped on a topical band-wagon. When the Archbishop of Canterbury made a strong statement last autumn on this subject, voicing his concern for our reckless disregard for nature, *The Times* ran an editorial entitled 'The Greening of the Archbishop'. However, my predecessor, Bishop John Bickersteth, who for many years had been an advocate for issues of conservation, quite rightly protested that the Archbishop was saying no more than the biblical tradition states!

The idea still persists that organized Christianity has only recently stumbled upon these truths. I will be arguing in this address that we have been as guilty as many other sections of our community in treating it too lightly, or in putting it lower down in our order of priorities than it ought to be; but it has never been entirely absent from Christian thought or theology. Indeed, as long ago as 1958 the Lambeth Conference of Bishops issued this Resolution:

> In relation to God's creation, over which he seems to exercise control, man is in danger of failing to recognize that he is a trustee, a steward, who must render account. This may be seen in his pollution of air, soil and ocean and in his scant disregard for the balance of nature or the needs of future generations and his tendency, without restraint, to use animal creation for his own ends.

Furthermore, as some of you here know, the diocese of Bath and Wells set up a working party in 1986 to set out our own policy. This was published in a useful report, *Our Relationship with the Whole of Creation* (1987). This has been studied in many parishes and has led to some changes of heart and attitudes.

It is clear despite this that not enough is being done, and the seriousness of the position is still not fully realized by the average person. Groups in our society such as Friends of the Earth, Greenpeace and the Green Party are to be congratulated for the energetic way they are drawing our attention to the issues involved. Yes, leading politicians may talk about the 'airy-fairy' Greens and seek to marginalize groups by such dismissive statements. Nonetheless, the very fact that no less a person than the Prime Minister speaks in such a way is a confession that green issues have intruded upon political life to such an extent that they can no longer be ignored!

Let me now build up my argument. First, let us look at *the Christian idea of creation*. The Christian faith has a very clear ideology of the created order. It is of nature created and hallowed by a personal God who pours into it his creativity and love. It is wholly hallowed and consecrated. The biblical tradition, while taking sin and the Fall seriously, does not consider the universe and the world as things to be exploited, but rather to be treated with respect. Mankind is charged with responsibility for the care of creation as a steward is given charge over the property of another. There are, for example, passages in the Old Testament which speak of a 'sabbath rest' for nature. I commend the book *God is Green* by Ian Bradley which sets out a useful outline of Christian thought on this subject.

It is a mistake, I submit, to go along with the Dominican Matthew Fox in denying the concepts of the Fall and sin. This appealing and influential writer condemns Augustinian spirituality – with what he believes is its over-concentration on the Fall and sinfulness – in favour of what he calls 'creation spirituality'. He believes that Augustinian thought is largely to be blamed for the split between Christian morality and nature. There is truth in what he argues, but not the whole truth. We create a wider chasm if the Christian view of humanity's sinfulness, wilfulness and downright evil is ever ignored.

It is all too self-evident that organized Christianity has not always followed the splendid theology which is there at the centre. There are probably many reasons for this and I shall mention only a few of the important ones. First was, no doubt, the over-spiritualizing of life with its assumption that the natural order was of trivial importance to our spiritual relationship with God. This world with all its concerns was thus seen as but an 'ante-room' of heaven. Thus physical and natural things were denigrated. A second reason was closely related to this, namely an anthropocentrism which came close to asserting that man could do whatever he liked with creation. It was tacitly assumed by everyone that every single thing existed for the benefit of humankind – nature was man's convenient larder or leisure bowl. It was there to be exploited.

Here are some illustrations of that attitude. Henry Moore argued that God created garden weeds to exercise the industry of man to dig them out! You may recall that in 1976 a Church of Scotland minister, defending his action in shooting two of Gavin Maxwell's adopted otter cubs as they were playing on the shore, argued that 'the Lord gave man control over the beasts of the field'. This anthropocentric attitude is not confined to Protestants alone. Even John Henry Newman wrote this about animals: 'We may use them, we may destroy them at our pleasure. For our own end, for our benefit or satisfaction.'

We may well express our enlightened horror at such ideas. For my part I am not condemning, I am illustrating the fact that the Christian symbiosis between nature and humankind, expressed so well in the Bible, has from time to time been replaced by man's domination of nature with disastrous consequences for both.

This moves me to my second point, *the desecration of creation*. We have to face the fact that we are not a nice species. I recall years ago visiting a nature trail with my then young family. We saw a sign saying, 'To the most dangerous creature of all'. We were curious. How exciting! So we followed the sign, and with some amusement found ourselves confronting a huge mirror! Yes, we are predators; we are consumers on an unprecedented scale in history. In nature, the numbers of the predator are always fewer than their prey, thus giving nature time and space to maintain control between species. Human life has achieved such a high density of population, however, and has such domination, that the structure of our environment is in danger of breaking down under the relentless punishment we are giving our habitat.

The problem comes in many forms, but for the sake of brevity let me concentrate on *pollution*. First, pollution caused by combustion. In spite of the fact that since the Clean Air Act of 1956, pollution caused by smoke has been greatly reduced to the benefit of those who live in the cities, we must not fool ourselves into thinking that there is no longer any problem. The facts point in the other direction. The effect of sulphur dioxide emissions by power stations and industrial concerns is a major environmental threat, causing acidification and what is called 'die-back' in trees. Last year, walking in a forest above Lake Geneva, I saw terrible evidence of this as acre after acre of trees seemed to be dying from the top down.

Then we can think of water pollution. Rivers have always been a dumping ground for man's unwanted waste. Nature has, of course, tremendous resilience in coping with abuse; even great quantities of waste can be broken down by the bacteria in the water. But there are limits, and we are told by scientists that those limits are being reached in our own time. We can easily understand why. High levels of waste will make it difficult for a river to absorb the quantities involved, reducing its ability to recycle waste, with the result that aquatic life dies and human life is threatened with disease.

Other types of pollution could be illustrated. In each case the same serious message is coming through – we are poisoning our environment, we are disrupting the interrelating ecosystems that form the background to human existence, we are endangering God's creation.

Now no one pretends that solutions are easy to find. The intention of this paper is not to blame, but to understand. I am not saying to the politician, 'You must get your act together.' I am not saying to the farmer, 'You must use fewer insecticides.' I am not saying to the consumer in all of us, 'You must eat less, drive less, enjoy life less.' To quote that well-known politician again, I am not interested in 'airy-fairy' solutions; but I am interested in promoting responsible attitudes to life.

So what can we do?

There are people who are convinced that the problem is so acute that lasting damage has already been done. One well-known thinker is the German theologian Jürgen Moltmann whose writings on this subject are of importance to anyone interested in issues of creation. He argues that the danger of an ecological collapse of the earth – what he calls 'ecological death' – is greater than the danger of a nuclear catastrophe. He cites in support of this the population explosion. In 1926, the year of his birth, 2 billion people inhabited this planet. By the year 2020 there will be 8 billion people living here. That is to say, within 100 years the human population will have quadrupled. The needs and waste of humanity have multiplied accordingly. Whatever we do, argues Moltmann, damage has been caused because of the irreversibility of the development of humanity.

However, while I believe Moltmann's case is unanswerable, it makes no difference to my contention that we are given certain responsibilities to ensure that we do something positive. The predator must become a repentant steward. How are we going to start this act of 'reformation'? We need to rediscover our symbiotic relationship with the rest of creation. The key word is *co-operation*. The human species is part of nature and apart from it. The idea that the rest of creation is here for our benefit makes no sense biologically, but the idea is so widespread in society and so deeply ingrained in our approach to life, that it gives rise to an arrogant and destructive 'hubris'. This 'separation from' approach is the root of such destructiveness because it is of the nature of the 'outsider' not to care. Why should he, is the shrugged reaction – I don't belong here, this is not my home. It may be the approach of the atheist for whom the whole of life is meaningless; it may be the approach of the over-spiritualizing theist for whom this world is irrelevant. No responsible Christian or, dare I say, responsible humanist could possibly endorse that view, however. From the Christian perspective we are 'insiders', part and parcel of God's design, and woe betide us if we take the position of the Creator.

Yet how do we co-operate? It is a great idea, we may think, but very hard to implement. We have to face the fact that economic factors and, all too often, short-term economic factors, shape attitudes to the environment. The factory, faced by demands from minority groups that it should not discharge its waste into the local river, will be unmoved by such considerations if its productivity and its economic survival depend upon keeping costs down.

This takes me into another key word and it is *education*. I am convinced that it should be the goal of every concerned person to share in that task of educating people to think and behave ecologically. This is beginning to happen through the exhortation as well as education received from Friends of the Earth and Greenpeace. I am delighted that our Government has taken this seriously enough to have a minister devoted to environmental issues. I am glad that universities are running courses on environmental biology. I am grateful to the BBC and independent TV stations for regular broadcasts which highlight conservation matters.

More can and ought to be done, however. The educative process has to begin sufficiently early in a person's life for it to have any real effect on attitudes, and I believe the challenge has to have the response of both parents and schools. The task of parents is to 'mentor' their children so that by example and instruction their children may capture a glimpse of the true values of life. The task of the school is to educate and to influence the growing mind of the child through knowledge. Frankly, I believe that it begins in an attitude to life which is almost mystical, if not religious, in its orientation and approach. I mean by this attitudes of wonder, reverence and awe, as we contemplate the beauty of the universe and note the fragility of its life-systems.

'Knowledge' is often associated with external forms of knowledge: of objective, dispassionate study which leads to theoretical commitment. I am arguing for something far more significant than that, and we might call it a case for *ecological morality*. Yes, we have all heard of personal morality and social moralities – but this is one that embraces the whole of reality. Its basis is that all life is to be valued and treated with respect; that the rhythm of life is something implanted by the Creator; that the different ecosystems have to be treasured, even when we regard them as hostile to human life itself. Their utilitarian contribution to our welfare should not, in other words, be our criterion as to whether they survive or not. An important element of such an ecological morality will include a style of ecological justice which is vigilant for a symbiosis of humanity and nature. An ecological reform of our societies will need to take into account, therefore, the compatibility of our innovations as much for our habitat as for ourselves.

We need a healthy recognition of the fact that we are a rather big-headed little species in a vast cosmos that can do without us, thank you very much! God did not depend upon us for his creation; indeed, I have heard it expressed rather forcefully that humankind is not one of God's better experiments! Time may well tell us whether that judgement is correct or not. For myself, I remain convinced that private morality cannot be divorced from public and environmental moralities and I predict that the politics of the future will have to lay greater stress on this area of life. Robert Paehlke's recent book *Environmentalism and the Future of Progressive Politics* is, I believe, an important and real contribution to this.

Finally, this leads me into *green disciplining*. This means bringing our behaviour into line with our theories, or, in Christian terms, it means making theology and disciplining one. I have no hesitation in saying that this implies all of us seeking a simpler lifestyle and making appropriate changes to the way we live, the things we eat, the way we travel, and so on. We should not assume that this means a retreat from the world into a monastery or a desert – not at all. But it will mean some form of acceptable lifestyle that will subject us to the discipline of God's world and the needs of his creation.

Now why should we do that? I have already mentioned the principal reason – that we are predators and our ravishing of the earth's resources, if continued at its present rate, will lead to disaster for our patient planet. There is also another reason. We live in a world in which one third of the population consumes two thirds of the world's resources. The Christian and the caring humanist cannot remain unconcerned for the plight of the people of the Third World who live so close to starvation. Among them are millions of our fellow Christians; but whether they are Christian or Muslim or whatever, they are fellow human beings and made in the image and likeness of God – and we have a responsibility for them.

So to the question: Is God green? The answer must be an emphatic and joyful 'yes'; greener than you or I will ever be! He calls us all to that relationship of stewardship which has been our calling ever since *homo sapiens* tended that first field. A mature Christian is in no doubt that God's concern for this world is greater than ours. He who valued life so much to enter it in the form of a human person must be committed to its survival. It is in the life and fragrance of that person, Jesus of Nazareth, that we have a pattern of care and love for all things which can be the basis for a discipleship that takes in a holistic approach to life.

9

Prayer – a Two-Way Conversation

Stoke Bishop, 15 February 1987

I have in my hand a wonderful book called *Children's Letters to God*. Here are some of the short prayers and letters addressed to God from small children:

> Dear God,
> Are you real? Some people don't believe it. If you are, you better do something quick.
> *Harriet Ann*

> Dear God,
> I love you God. During arithmetic a dog came in.
> *Krista*

> Dear God,
> Are boys better than girls? I know you are one, but try to be fair.
> *Sylvia*

> Dear God,
> We got a lot of religion in our house. So don't worry about us.
> *Teddy*

Although the authors call them letters they are in fact a form of communication we call prayer. They reflect different types of prayer: praising, thanking, accusing, talking, asking.

In this sermon on prayer, I want us to think about prayer as a two-way conversation in which we talk to God and in which we listen to him as well. I think it will help us to hold on to what I am going to say if we keep in mind two pictures: a hallway of a house, and a telephone.

Let us look first at prayer as a *hallway*. Have you ever considered how important the hallway of your home is? It is far more than just an accidental entrance to your home. It is the place where you greet people who have the right to step over the doormat but no right to go any further. It is the place which our neighbours find so fascinating that, in spite of our invitation to enter the living room, they say, 'I won't stay a moment', but find that they stay thirty minutes! I am sure you have neighbours like that, too. The main thing about a hallway, however, is that you cannot go anywhere in the house without passing through it. It gathers up the movement of the house as we pass from kitchen to living room or dining room, or kitchen to bedrooms.

I find this an illuminating analogy of the real purpose of prayer. Prayer is far more than a shopping list, or an incidental five minutes at the end of a busy day. In the life of a maturing Christian it is that space I give in quiet thought, reflection and meditation. It is that time when I gather up all that has happened in my day, and all that is going to happen today. Understood in this way, then, prayer is not something I do but something I am. Just as a hallway has no meaning on its own – after all, you cannot buy hallways without the rest of the building ('nice hallway to sell, hardly ever used') – so prayer has no meaning on its own. Prayer, you see, in this sense, is what we *are*. It does not stand alone. It is the innermost centre of what we are, the place where we are most authentically ourselves.

This form of prayer, then, gathers up all our experiences and takes them to the King of Kings, and we think about them in his presence – all the hurts, all the joys, all that stops us becoming the kind of persons we feel called to be. I would urge anyone to find space in a busy day to pray in this kind of way. For some, the morning is the best time; for others perhaps late evening. Perhaps it is as you travel to work, or as you take the dog out for a walk, or as you walk on the Downs, or when you have that quiet morning cup of coffee. Perhaps it is when you drive your car – as long as you don't close your eyes! It is 'space to be', when you gather up everything that crosses the threshold of your life and where it is interpreted in the light of your walk with God.

It may be that in your hallway is my second image of prayer, the *telephone*, that irritating friend whose shrill cry has to be answered. Perhaps you have had telephone problems of late and you are waiting for the Telecom engineer. It is good to know that God's telephone never breaks down. He is always available. The telephone is my link with the outside world. We may complain about it many times, but think of its wonderful facility of allowing us to phone that relative in the United States, or a friend a few miles away, or the butcher, or our business, and so on.

On the phone we talk and we listen. Sometimes our teen-agers talk to their boyfriends and girlfriends for hours on the phone. Mystified parents, who ought to know better, ask: 'What took you so long? Surely you didn't have that much to say to one another? After all, you are seeing him in ten minutes.' Then they smile because they know you really ought to have known better. 'Can't you remember, Mum and Dad, what it was like to just talk, and gossip, and say sweet things without saying really *anything*, and yet saying all the import-ant things?' Isn't that going to the very heart of prayer – a two-way conversation in which we talk and in which we do some listening as well?

'Well!' says someone, 'I know what you mean by talking to God but what do you mean by listening to him? Quite frankly, I need a guide because otherwise all I'll be listening to are my hopes and fears and desires.'

Yes, I understand that point of view. God, however, has given two very important guides to help the Christian as he or she listens. The first is the Holy Spirit, and the second is the Bible which is his tool. You see, each of us has to make sure that we are listening to God's voice and not our own fantasies. So how do we do it?

To some degree we must all find the system best for our-selves, but let me tell you what I do. I find my listening springs best out of reading a few verses from Scripture. It does not have to be a long passage, it may only be a verse. Let me take one from the passage read to us: Philippians 4. Let us imagine that you are studying this in your room and you read verse 6: 'Have no anxiety about anything, but in everything by prayer and supplication with thanksgiving let your requests be made known to God.' As you start to think about the things that make you anxious you realize that the passage is telling you not to be anxious but to pray with thanksgiving! Now what is God saying to me through this passage? . . . and you find yourself ruminating on the things you are anxious about, and you start to relate this to the person you are. Is there something here in this passage that should influence your behaviour today? Let me give you a personal illustration.

About six months ago I was very cross with a colleague who had, in my opinion, acted irresponsibly. I remember approaching the theological college quite determined to 'sort him out'. As I approached the college the phrase from this passage: 'in everything by prayer and supplication with thanksgiving' flashed through my mind. I started to meditate on that verse in relation to my argument with my colleague. I imagined God saying something like this: 'So you are going to sort him out, are you? Begin with thanking me for him; look at him as a person as important to me as you are.' I did so. I started to thank God for this colleague of mine and his gifts and commitment. As you will have guessed, my attitude towards him changed, so that when the frank speaking happened that day it was in the context of love and acceptance of him as a person.

So prayer as *talking* and *listening* needs to be an important element in our daily walk with God. Don't skimp on it, because the experience of great Christians has been that without it we cannot grow into Christian maturity. Francis de Sales, a great Christian writer, used to say: 'Half an hour's daily listening is essential except when you are very busy and then a full hour is necessary.' An interesting thought, because he turns on its head our usual temptation to crowd prayer out when we are busy.

Now the consequences of seeing prayer as a hallway and as a telephone are momentous.

First, we will see prayer as a natural way of talking with God. It is the language of the heart in tune with its Maker. It is the place where we gather up all the experiences of life and think about them. As a hallway, it is the place where I invite the good Lord to step over the threshold and talk with me. 'Come on in and help me make sense of this life I live.' In a very real way, I have found, it is the only place where things have been really understood for the first time.

Second, when prayer is seen as a conversation with a very dear friend, we begin to understand prayer as far, far more than just asking God for a hand-out. We begin to understand Jesus' prayer in the Garden of Gethsemane, 'Not my will, but thine, be done' (Luke 22.42). As that little poem puts it:

> He answered prayer not in the way I sought,
> Nor in the way that I thought he ought,
> But in his own good way, and I could see,
> He answered in the fashion best for me.

Third, prayer in the light of the Bible and guided by the Holy Spirit will change me: change my attitudes, make me more like the person God wants me to be. That, surely, ought to be our ambition.

10

Sacraments in the Spiritual Life

To the Irish School of Ecumenics,
the Corrymeela Community, Northern Ireland.
Seventh Clergy Conference, 10 May 1988

You will notice no definite article before the word 'sacraments' and this gives me a little liberty to begin my address reasonably broadly. When we use the word 'sacrament', what do we mean? Within the tradition I represent, the classic definition is that of 'outward and visible sign of an inward and spiritual grace'. The word 'sign', however, needs careful thought. Do we mean a symbol which only 'represents' a reality – like a road sign – or do we mean a sign which actually embodies or conveys, in some shape or form, the reality to which it points? Paul Tillich was in no doubt, and in a famous phrase remarked: 'A sacrament partakes of the reality it conveys.'

I have been asked to speak on this subject from the viewpoint of the Evangelical tradition and I am glad to do so, but with the following cautionary note. While I owe much to that tradition and trust that I am still *persona grata* within it, in many respects I have gone beyond Evangelical thought on matters to do with the Church and sacraments. Others, then, will have to judge whether my views expressed here are consonant with that tradition. I trust they are. At any rate I am aware that a rising generation of Evangelical students and scholars are in general sympathy with the views I espouse.

My starting point is Christ. For Christians there is only one primordial and basic sacrament, and that is Christ himself. In speaking of Christ as 'sacrament' I am endorsing the witness of the Church in history which has seen, in the incarnation of God's Son, the sacramental manifestation of God the Father himself. 'He that has seen me', Jesus said to Philip, 'has seen the Father.' I suggest that all our sacraments are derivative sacraments, because they all originate from the source of God's life in and through his Son.

Our response is, of course, twofold – encounter and worship – and these are inseparably connected.

Let us explore the first of these words – 'encounter'. How do I encounter God in such a way that I can call the meeting sacramental? First, I must recall that Christ has first encountered us as Saviour and Lord. In his life, death and resurrection we are made right with God. We cannot love God with our whole hearts, souls and minds. Christ, however, has and does. It is therefore Christ who presents us to the Father, and our salvation derives from him. Salvation is not, though, a past event. Our total experience of life is a firm refutation of that; we know the reality within us of failure, of sinfulness and consequently of the need for forgiveness and restoration. That is why within the Evangelical tradition there is the emphasis on the believer being *simul justus et peccator*, simultaneously made right with God but still sinful.

Second, encounter with God never takes place in a vacuum. In our case it takes place in the family of Christ's body, the Church, the location in which the sacramental is normally expressed. Now this may sound an anathema to some Evangelical ears because for some the Church is but a secondary fact in Christian truth, coming a long way after personal faith and experience. For myself I have to reject this way of contemplating the Church because of its individualistic bias. The New Testament knows nothing of a separation of the individual from the Church; to be a Christian is to belong to the body; to be baptized into Christ is to be incorporated into his people. I have no hesitation, therefore, in speaking of the Church itself as 'sacrament' in the sense that here is this broken body which is called by his name, I meet him and he indwells it. He is present in its ministry, in its preaching, in its sacraments, in its prayers and in its witness.

Let us now come to the second response, namely worship. In this Church where I encounter the Triune God I am called to worship with my whole being. I have a strong feeling that in all our communities our worship falls a long way short of New Testament and Patristic practice. Let me mention just one aspect of worship which I call *worship as rehearsal*. For us, worship is merely our duty to respond to God's love by a discipline which, for most Christians, amounts to one visit to the local church a week. There, in predictable manner, we sing our hymns and say our prayers. Good; but, I submit, it is not good enough. Is not worship more than that? Should it not be in a vital and vivid way a recital and rehearsal of God's plan of salvation? Should not worship set forth the gospel and proclaim the faith of the Church? In ecumenical circles of late we have been reminded that 'remembering' in the biblical context was far more than simply recalling to mind what God had done in the past. This word *anamnesis* meant the past invading the present, so that here the past was relived and appropriated.

Worship, you see, is the action of the entire congregation who together proclaim what God has done and what he continues to do; we feed on his word – sacrament and Scripture – and are strengthened by his Spirit and sustained by mutual fellowship. Furthermore, although this action takes place in a local congregation, it is the worship of the whole people of God – the living and the dead, the Church militant and triumphant, for together they constitute the body of Christ.

It is in this context of *anamnesis* (of 'recalling' and 'reliving' the events of Christ's victory) that I wish to talk about the role of the sacraments in the spiritual life. In its broadest sense, we can talk of the 'sacramentality' of life, in that God may be seen, experienced and discovered in the normality of life. We should be suspicious of any school of thought which separates spirituality from the natural and human as if God comes to people independent of this context. While it is the Catholic Christian who will most naturally speak in this way, it is not unknown for the Evangelical Christian to make statements which come fairly close to that. Listen to him talking about his moment of conversion when at a certain event he 'asked Jesus into his heart'. That moment and place can never be expunged from his memory. Similarly, the Evangelical can speak of an encounter with the words of the text of Scripture as though God has spoken directly to him. On a broader canvas, many of us can think of moments of encounter, of blessing, of poetry, of art, of music, of sunsets and dawns which were to us deeply sacramental.

For us all, however, the two dominical sacraments stand out

from all the rest – namely baptism and Holy Communion. The former represents the once-for-all giving of spiritual life, and the latter the regular repetition of the saving events of the cross and resurrection. It is this last sacrament which, by its very nature, is deeply significant to the Christian. For the rest of this address I will describe its role for me in my spiritual journey. Hopefully I will be speaking on behalf of Evangelicals and many Anglicans.

First, *it is the focal point of forgiveness.* The Eucharist is the sacrament of salvation and, as such, it declares the work of Christ as he fulfils the Father's will and draws all people to God. Sadly, this representation of our salvation has been the source of the rift between two historic Communions as both have misheard or misunderstood what the other has been trying to say. The Protestant Christian has too quickly jumped to the conclusion that Catholicism regards the Holy Communion service as a work of salvation whereby the priest offers afresh the offering of Christ and pleads for salvation. The Catholic Christian has perhaps decided that the Protestant sees the sacrament merely as a memorial service, witnessing to an event in the past.

Both views, of course, are distortions and we need to listen again to what the other is really trying to say. In this, the statement by the Anglican-Roman Catholic International Commission (ARCIC) II, 'Salvation and the Church', is a major breakthrough because theologians from the Roman Catholic and Anglican Communions were able to state together the 'once-for-all' offering of Christ on the cross, and that we are not saved *by* good works but *for* good works. Section 27 expresses it well: 'This once-for-all atoning work of Christ, realized and experienced in the life of the Church and celebrated in the Eucharist, continues the free gift of God which is proclaimed in the gospel.'

I speak personally when I say that for me the Eucharist represents God's powerful declaration that I am 'ransomed, healed, restored and forgiven'. It does not *of itself* forgive, rather it sets forth what God has done in Christ. However, since it is more than a mere sign, it partakes of the reality it signifies and is a means of grace through which the atoning work of Christ is made effective in the life of the Christian.

Second, for me *the sacrament of Holy Communion is a focal*

point of feeding. I must deny a 'real absence'. It is common for Evangelicals to speak as if they are denying a 'real presence' but this is far from the case. Having taught many generations of Evangelical students, I am aware that many come to theological colleges with inchoate views concerning the nature of the Eucharist. However most of them have a strong sense that in this celebration of the Church, Christ himself is present and feeds with Word and Sacrament those who come to him through faith.

This is the reality for me. In this sacrament I meet the risen Christ; I feed on him and rely on his promise that, as the people of God meet to recall him in his death and passion, so we are able to take the elements and say 'This is my body . . . This is my blood of the new covenant'. I don't wish to reopen sterile arguments about the meaning of 'is-ness'. Surely, five hundred years of argument have convinced most reasonable people of the vacuity of this debate. Many of us from experience wish to say something like this: 'Lord, I do not have the ability to comprehend how you feed me through such simple gifts as this piece of bread or wafer or that sip of wine – but I know you do!' As the ARCIC I statement on Eucharistic doctrine puts it so well:

> The sacramental body and blood of the Saviour are present as an offering to the believer awaiting his welcome. When this offering is met by faith, a life-giving encounter results. Through faith Christ's presence – which does not depend on the individual's faith in order to be the Lord's real gift of himself to his Church – becomes no longer just a presence for the believer, but also a presence with him. (Section 8)

I am aware that there will be those, Catholics and Evangelicals, who will regret the vagueness of such language. They would prefer the vigour of language which either asserted the fact of 'real presence' in words which clothed the mode of his coming with an unmistakable reality, or which spoke of a 'real absence' in order to preserve the purity of Christ's coming to the heart of the believer in faith. For myself, both these extremes are unsatisfactory. Not only because both are unbiblical but because both misunderstand the way language is used

when we grope to make sense of experiencing God. The theological term for this is *analogia fidei*; that is to say, when we
talk of eternal verities we have to resort to pictures, stories and
other analogical expressions. The Bible is full of such analogies and pictorial expressions which point beyond themselves. Yet I must resist both the temptation of identifying
word with reality and that of separating word from reality. All
our language is a groping after a reality which we already
possess in part.

Perhaps it is in this context that Evangelicals and Catholics
have to look afresh at the troublesome problem of speaking of
the sacrament as a 'sacrifice'. Historically and theologically,
of course, it is not and can never be. As 'sacrament' it *stands
for* the sacrifice of the cross through which we were brought
near to God. Analogically the sacrament can certainly be
understood as 'sacrifice' in the sense that if it partakes of the
reality it represents, the 'once-for-all' sacrifice of Calvary is
applied to us as we celebrate the victory as well as the mystery
of the cross.

Third, *the Eucharist is the focal point of fellowship.* When we
come together for worship it is as the body of Christ, *to be* the
body of Christ and *to feed on* the body of Christ. In the light of
this awesome fact, how can we treat our membership of that
body so lightly? Yet our *koinōnia* (fellowship) so often falls
short of the unity Christ desires. I think of this with particular
reference to the local community and the wider community.

The application to the local community is one that I put as
a challenge to all: How can we help people to take seriously
membership in the Eucharistic community of faith? If the
Eucharist is essential for our spiritual growth, how may we all
integrate this most solemn and sacred of sacraments with
other vital elements in our experience? For example, how may
Evangelicals integrate it with their emphasis on the word
expressed in preaching and Bible study? How may Catholics
ensure that the Eucharist does not become separated from the
salvation it witnesses to in Christ?

If the Eucharist is that important, a second question follows:
How can we help others to understand its theological significance as well as its mystery to which we subject ourselves in
humility?

The application to the wider community brings us to the

purpose of our gathering in this place dedicated to unity. If the sacrament of Holy Communion is the sacrament of reconciliation, of unity, of God making peace through the blood of his cross, then we must face the fact that this sacrament witnesses to our deep divisions, our brokenness and hurt. None of our Churches is therefore a 'whole' Communion as a result. We may secretly take pride in our traditions and truth, but we are deficient as long as others are left outside in the cold and unable to share with us the sacrament of the Lord.

I am nonetheless a man of hope. Jürgen Moltmann once said so memorably: 'The nearer we come to Christ, the nearer we come together.' It is my hope and conviction that as we journey closer to him we shall find ourselves travelling with others and imperceptibly growing together into his beauty and likeness, and away from the ugliness and bitterness which has dogged the history of our Communions.

11

A Pilgrim at Walsingham

In 1988 the Bishop led a diocesan pilgrimage to Walsingham,
Norfolk. He gave the following three talks.

I. A Home that is Always Open

Here in Walsingham is commemorated the home of Jesus. In this church we have a striking and unusual likeness of a home. Are we not being reminded in a very distinctive yet emphatic way that this ought to be the nature of the Church?

A home is the very heart of life. Nothing can be finer, greater and more influential than a loving home. However, nothing can be crueller and more oppressive than one without love. Many of our blessings and our scars emanate from our homes. Here in this place we are being encouraged to come home to God's dwelling place. The actual context in which we meet is not important; it is only a symbol of God's dwelling among his people. Having said that, this place has been made 'valid through prayer' and can be seen as a sacrament of God's coming to us through the demands of human life.

God chose Mary to create a home for his Son. Why Mary? We don't know; but God never does things accidentally. He plans and prepares people to receive his grace and love.

I want to let you in on a somewhat embarrassing secret, which is now a secret no longer! I had been something like eighteen years in the ordained ministry before I preached my first sermon on Mary. Somehow the Protestant part of me could not find it right to speak of her place in God's order of salvation because I was afraid of her obscuring the central place of Jesus Christ in his Church. What changed my way of approaching things? Above all, it was the Bible. If we take Scripture seriously, Mary is there as part of the story. Without her, or someone like her, the story would have been completely different.

First, I saw that she was *chosen*, and that for all time 'all generations will call [her] blessed' (Luke 1.48). Indeed, the angel hails her, 'O favoured one!' (Luke 1.28), and later in the birth narratives Elizabeth salutes her: 'Blessed are you among women' (Luke 1.42). It would be wrong, then, to push Mary to the circumference of the Christian story. Her place is in the centre.

Second, I began to see why she was honoured in this way. I saw her *humility*. She entered into the shame of bearing God's Son and even ran the risk of being called a loose woman. She entered upon the slow crucifixion of seeing her son take the lonely, sad and inevitable road to his cross. As the handmaid of the Lord, most of the time she could only be there, watching helplessly. I began to see that my fear about Mary obscuring Christ was not soundly based as long as I keep to the parameters of Scripture. The advice recorded in John's Gospel is always worth following: 'Do whatever he tells you' (John 2.5). True Marian theology is truly Christ-centred.

Third, I saw her *availability*. She gave her consent to God's will. She was willing to be used by him and the outrageous request received the obedient, 'Let it be to me according to your word' (Luke 1.38).

Fourth, I saw her as *an example of God's grace*. There is nothing in the biblical account to suggest that Mary was extraordinary in any way. There is nothing to suggest that she was very clever, very holy, very gifted or very beautiful. Although tradition has assumed that she was some if not all of those things, we have no way of knowing. But that only adds to the wonder of the story that God took a willing young woman and poured into her his grace and love. The best definition I know of grace is: God's Riches At Christ's Expense. The One who took up his abode in Mary was the One who sustained her, kept her and made her holy.

It was Mary who, with her husband Joseph – also a striking and impressive example of God's grace – made of a simple house in Nazareth a home for the King of Kings.

What does a home signify to you?

Belonging

Observe the difference between the behaviour of children in their own home and that of friends who enter. Even though we may say, 'Make yourself at home', we might be a little taken aback if they took us at our word and kicked off their shoes, lounged around on the settee, helped themselves to our coffee, tea, larder and even our wine! There is a real difference between those who belong to the home because they have a natural relationship with the parents, and those who don't.

What does that say to us who are Christians, who belong to God by reason of our baptism and our confession? Let me illustrate this by introducing to you a man whom I shall call Tom, who was a member of my congregation in Durham. Tom was a very able businessman and a very keen Evangelical Christian. He was always zealous in good works, always regular at worship and a key member of the church. At work he was a high flier and his salary was commensurate with his ability.

One day Tom came to see me and poured out a story which told me the other side of his ambitious, over-achieving self. He was the product of a broken home and therefore a single-parent child. His mother was ambitious for her boy, and her ambition took the form of constantly encouraging, rebuking and endlessly telling him how he could improve. As time went on the comments became less encouraging and more accusing, so that at the age of forty-five, in my study, he told me how he felt a failure and as a Christian unable to understand God as a God of love. God to him was a figure of terror, of impossible standards. How extraordinary, I thought as we talked together, that this man's theological understanding of justification by faith – in which he believed passionately – had no echo whatsoever in his life. Then I began to see Tom's sad plight. The shadow side of his success was that of failure, watered by the constant accusing refrain that 'You are not good enough; you could do better; you will never get on if you don't try; God will not accept you if you don't try harder . . .'

There was no easy solution to Tom's problem. That meeting was only the beginning of a long series of meetings, retreats and counselling sessions which formed the stepping stones for a return to an authentic Christian experience. He began to see that God was not a tyrant but a loving Father; he began to see that the Christian life was not a series of impossible demands to satisfy the whims of an unreasonable employer; he began to see that he was welcome because of who he was, and not on the basis of what he could achieve.

I happen to know that there are many Toms in the Christian Church. If you would count yourself as one of them, can I suggest that you reflect on the fact that as Christians we are not only welcome in this home but we belong here.

Freedom and discipline

God has no favourites. We are all special to him, and he longs for each of us to enter into the space and privileges of his home. The mention of privileges, however, brings together two seeming opposites: freedom and discipline.

We have freedom to enjoy the space that God gives to us in his family. He gives us that space to grow into the maturity he wants from each of us: freedom to think, freedom to pray in our own way, freedom to worship according to our temperament and inclination.

We must remember, however, that God is never indulgent. He does not misuse freedom, and he does not expect us to either. The right use of freedom leads to the Christian discipline that we call 'holiness'. Although this is often construed as 'thou shalt not do this', or 'thou shalt not do that', holiness is really Christian discipline for the service of Christ. It is accepting the lifestyle of Christ so that we may be usable for God's glory. It is using our time, our talents and our money for God and his mission. There is very much a pattern of 'holy worldliness' about Christian discipline. Well did Dag Hammarskjøld say that 'the road to holiness necessarily passes through the world of action'. Well did the Book of Common Prayer put it succinctly when it spoke of the relationship between us and God: 'Whose service is perfect freedom'. This is a perfect picture of responsible parenthood, whether we are talking about human or divine parenthood. A good parent does not let his or her child do anything; there have to be proper guidelines, firm but loving admonition at times and clear but gentle encouragement. That is God's way with us, too.

Let us return to our pilgrimage. What might this theme, 'a home that is always open' mean to us?

Because God's home is always open, it means that we are always welcome and there is always forgiveness. God is giving us space to present himself to our hearts as a God of love but at the same time as a God who wants us to grow into his likeness. There are things in all our lives that displease him: misplaced ambition, wrong relationships, lack of prayerfulness, slackness in spiritual things, and so on. We all have a great deal of business to do with our heavenly Father and it is in the security of God's home that we can know that we belong and are special.

Max Warren, the great Christian leader and General Secretary of the Church Missionary Society, wrote of the home in this way:

> A home is the treasury of God
> where purity, beauty and joy
> are shared, for his purposes, inviolate.
> For a home is in itself the triumph of God
> banishing night and chaos and necessity,
> indwelling this lifeless clay
> with the Spirit divine of freedom and joy.

II. A Well that Never Runs Dry

If you ever get the chance to go to Nazareth you will be shown a well with the sign over it, 'St Mary's Well'. It was very possibly from that actual spring that Mary would have made daily journeys to fetch water. Perhaps, also, as a young boy Jesus himself might have been sent on errands to fill the pitcher. We might speculate further and say that they probably lived very close to the well because of the importance of water in the life of a Middle Eastern family.

Here at Walsingham there is a well. Today's theme will serve us satisfactorily as a basis for our meditation, because water has had a long association with such images of healing, blessing and anointing.

Let me tell you of the images that spring to my mind when we talk about water.

The reality of God's blessing
We are not surprised that water became the symbol of baptism

because of its associations with ordinary things like washing and refreshment. For the early Church, however, water was not just an image, but a dramatic and essential element in the blessing that God was going to give. Water for the Eastern mind was a very precious gift of God because it spelt the difference between life and death. Abundance of it represented laughter and joy; scarcity represented suffering and even death.

So here is a good place for us to begin. Water to you and me is so ordinary. We take it for granted. Yet that is where we begin with God: his providential care for each of us and his provision for each of our lives. I gave you yesterday the analogy of the home, and now we can imagine Mary bustling about the home with water for washing, for cooking and for cleaning. Each of these is a symbol of a deeper reality for us in the home of Christ.

An aspect of this is found in John 2.1-11. This familiar story about the wedding feast at Cana of Galilee points to the deeper reality there is to be found in Christ. Three significant things are to be seen in the story.

First, there is the embarrassment about the wine. Half way through the feast the wine runs out. We can all imagine the disgrace this would have caused. Whatever the reason, it was a most serious problem.

Second, Mary was there of her own right, and the fact that she is mentioned first probably indicates that she knew the family very well. She it is who mentions the embarrassment to Jesus. The conversation is curious and rather contrived and, like most of the conversations in John's Gospel, is Christocentric – that is, it points to the mystery and glory of Christ. 'They have no wine,' Mary said to Jesus. 'O woman, what have you to do with me?' retorted Jesus. 'My hour has not yet come' (John 2.3-4). We could paraphrase it to read: 'Mother, can't you see that this is not the time for my mission and nature to be revealed?' Like many a mother faced with the apparent intransigence of her child, she ignored the rebuff and gave the servants the best advice any of us could receive: 'Do whatever he tells you' (John 2.5).

The third significant thing in the story is, of course, the miracle itself. Jesus takes the water jars, wine is drawn from the village well and the water is changed.

So water for me represents the ordinariness of life which Jesus can take and make very special. Never despise ordinary things – the ordinary in yourself or in others. Never cheapen the wonder of the commonplace in life. God is able to take the common in you and me and make it a sacrament of blessing for others. Indeed, sacrament is the key word because it is a symbol of the reality to which it points but of which it also partakes. In a wonderful and mysterious way, when God's grace touches a person's life, the ordinary is irradiated with the glory of Christ making us 'grace-full'.

God's presence with his people

Our theme is 'A well that never runs dry' – and it never runs dry because it represents God's presence with us. When we use the phrase 'God with us' we mean, of course, the *incarnation*. I want to develop this theme for a while because it is central within this place of Walsingham. Incarnation means God becoming one of us, born of Mary; but there are some disconcerting features in the story which we need to observe and reflect upon.

First, it is a real incarnation. This is no pretend story, but one that stresses real earthiness – God's coming to the profane and ending the separation between sacred and secular. As I have reminded groups before now, the reality of incarnation has been central to Catholic spirituality and practice; that is not so true of other traditions. As one born a 'Cockney' I can tell you of the great Catholic priests who lived among the poor of the East End of London – and loved them into the Kingdom of God. Like that lovely story about Brother Andrew among tramps and vagrants, leading the singing and picking fleas off his cassock as they sang quite innocently: 'Count your blessings, name them one by one!'

Even if our ministries do not take that form of living as radically as that, incarnation does challenge each of us to apply the message of Christ. 'Connect,' screams the gospel, 'don't just talk about the faith, live it and die for it!'

Second, incarnation stresses the pathway of weakness and even failure that is the pattern of discipleship. The incarnational model of Mary and Jesus stresses that it is our very weakness which may become a tool for the Kingdom. Paul says in 1 Corinthians 1.27 that 'God chose what is foolish in the world to shame the wise'. While no doubt Paul was think-ing of the uncomplicated Christian message compared with the sophisticated philosophies of his day, and of the simple slaves and ordinary people who were joining the Christian family, he might have had the Lord's background in mind as well. How strange that God chose the Jews, and how extraor-dinary that he placed the Messiah in an ordinary Jewish home in a backwater place among the yokels of Galilee of the Gen-tiles!

Between ourselves, I sometimes find myself struggling with the reality of living in a Church which patently does not live out the implications of all this. Our Church often measures things in terms of worldly success, and not in terms of the humility of weakness and failure. Acceptance so often seems to rest with what we are and our place in society. 'Are you a success and with a healthy bank balance? Welcome!' 'Are you energetic with lots of ideas? Welcome!' 'Are you able to become a youth leader? Churchwarden? Then come on in!' 'Oh, I see, you are poor, weak, you don't have many GCSEs. I note you are getting on a bit. Sorry, we cannot find a place for you in the Christian ministry.'

How that contrasts with the message we preach! Now I am not, of course, challenging the excellence that God requires from us all but I am challenging a tendency to overthrow the radical message of incarnation. The famous Curé d'Ars would have failed an ACCM on academic grounds and St Paul would have been rejected for other reasons. Yet I see from Church history the many glorious illustrations of God's weak people. Take some of the Lord's disciples – Andrew, James, John, and even Peter himself. Take such people as Gladys Aylward, D.L. Moody, Mother Teresa and many other 'average' people whose lives were made remarkable through the grace of God. John Henry Newman knew his Church history when he wrote:

> Few tho' the faithful and fierce the foe,
> Yet weakness is aye Heaven's might.

Fellow pilgrims, the wonderful reality of incarnation is a message to us all that God can take the foolish things of this life and make us rich vessels for his use. The water can still be changed into the wine of his presence.

In my garden at Wells I have a wonderful well – indeed, there are five of them and the city of Wells derives its name from the five springs in the Palace grounds. The extraordinary thing about the place is its ordinariness. If you were to visit it you would be struck by the quietness of the small pool. No great torrents of water, no spectacular waterfalls, no deafening roars of waters disgorging their immense might. Indeed, if you are lucky, on a clear day you might just be able to see the spring bubbling up at the bottom of the pond. Yet from that very still place immense power emerges. Thousands of gallons of water per minute flow from underground streams which pour from the tranquil pool to form the moat and run into the gutters of Wells and into the many little streams around, irrigating the fields with their dancing life and wonderful presence.

Surely that is a picture of what God longs to do with your life and mine. We think of the desert of modern life with the concentration on material possessions and its resultant poverty. We consider the dryness of the Church as it tends to be too often a shadow image of that world. Our God can still take the ordinary and make it extraordinary. He is able to take the weakness of our present experience and say to our hearts: 'Look, don't despise yourself. You are special, you are made in my image and likeness. Let me take hold of that weakness of yours and let me change your water into wine.'

III. A Fire that will Never Go Out

I don't know about you, but I cannot conceive of a home without a fire. Even in these days of gas and electric fires it is quite unusual for a living room to be bereft of a fireplace. It is normally the central point of a home and around it gather the family as we meet for fellowship, fun and general chit-chat. Although we are not told it, Mary's home would certainly have had a fire in the one and only downstairs room, and there the Holy Family would have met to eat and to share together.

What images spring to your mind when you think of fire? In the New Testament, fire is a principal symbol of the Holy Spirit, and that is what I want to talk about now.

To begin with, let me remind you that there is a very profound link between the Virgin Mary and the Holy Spirit. Right from the beginning of the Christian story we can see the Spirit at work. He came upon Mary and anointed her to be the mother of the Lord. There could be no miracle of the virginal conception without the work of the Third Person of the Trinity. He is the unsung and unseen dynamic in the infancy narratives. That same Spirit, of course, empowered Jesus for his rich ministry and led John the Baptist to tell others of the One who would baptize people with the Holy Spirit and with 'fire'. And, as we know so well, the Holy Spirit fell on the day of Pentecost with tongues as of fire.

For Mary, however, the coming of the Spirit was not a comfortable experience! Anyone who has romantic ideas of what it must have been like for great women and men to be filled with God's Spirit should think again if the story of Mary is anything to go by. The empowering of the Spirit for her took the form of risk, misunderstandings and downright difficulties. 'The Comforter', once remarked Cardinal Suenens, 'is given, not to make us comfortable, but to make us disciples.'

What aspects of the Spirit's work do we see when we explore the image of fire?

Holiness and clarity of truth
I wonder if I may offer some thoughts on this theme as I reflect on the situation facing Catholic Christians in our Church today. I am keenly aware, as you know, of the many Catholics whose faith and commitment have been badly shaken and disturbed in recent days, particularly over the ordination of women to the priesthood. I can say this with sympathy and love even though I am, as many know, entirely supportive of the ordination of women. This stand does not make me blind to the distress others feel or to the disillusionment that this issue causes. The recent nomination of a woman as Assistant Bishop of Massachusetts, and the remarks of one diocesan bishop that 'the ordination of women to the priesthood must be achieved at practically any cost' will cause great despair and lead to grave questioning of all that the Church of England has stood for. What is going on? What can be done? Is the fire going out in Catholicism generally?

It is important to have a wide backcloth when considering these problems. We in the Church of England are not alone among Christians in having daunting questions to resolve. The Roman Catholic Communion has many issues that it seeks to resolve: the urgent problem of falling vocations for the priesthood, the problem of a celibate priesthood, the Lefebvre schism, the tension between local churches and the Roman See, and so on. Other denominations, too, are wrestling with similar problems, but all of us are, in reality, dealing with the same central problem: What is, in essence, the kernel of Christian truth that is non-negotiable, and what is expendable? What is a 'first-order' issue and what are 'second-' and even 'third-order' questions?

There is something about a fire that reminds me of holiness and truth. A fire burns away the dross; the dirt and old paint are burnt away leaving the sharpness and clarity of the original metal. Similarly, on retreats such as this one, the fire of the Holy Spirit has an opportunity to burn away the dross of the Church and even of doctrine that may obscure the faith that is central to all we believe and hope for. The ecclesiasticism that so often gets in the way of the gospel; the temporal concerns of church politics that take up so much time; the fussiness of much of church life; our obsession with 'churchy' things – all these and more are aspects of additions that are really secondary concerns.

God has a way on retreats such as this of bringing home to us the challenge of a first-order question: 'Do you love me in the way Mary loved me and allowed herself to be used for my mission?' I hope we shall leave here with a deeper love and, if I dare suggest it, a more confident love.

We might say, however: 'If the fire burns away the dross and leaves the real thing behind, what is the nature of that original?' I am prepared to answer at once: 'Why Christ, of course, and our love for him which is fed and watered by the prayers of his people in his Church.' This has been central to the Catholic tradition as we well know. Take the famous Curé d'Ars, Jean-Baptiste Vianney. His is the remarkable story of a young man with hardly any academic ability. Today we might say that he was a little 'thick'. There is simply no way he would have been accepted for training in our Church – and that is perhaps a tragedy. God nonetheless blessed him and used him. He made the priesthood and exercised a distinguished ministry. His secret? He was a man for whom Catholicity was reduced to its Evangelical essentials – the love of God, a burning desire that people should know and love his Saviour, and a great belief in the power of prayer. Although a faithful man of his own Church, everything was subsumed under these Evangelical essentials.

The crisis of Catholicism today is a question of direction: Where is Catholic renewal to go from here? In spite of the many things it has achieved over the last hundred years – and we have all been shaped by that – it has got itself boxed in by one issue. As I find myself an outsider at this point, I can only put to you another question: Are you really sure that the issue of the ordination of women is so fundamental to the gospel that you would leave your Church and, in some cases, surrender your ministries on that point? Is that in essence a central datum of Catholicity?

So where is Catholic renewal to go from here? Only you can answer that. I would hope that you would see beyond that, and issues like it, the primary claims of Christ in his Church, to love him and to promote him as Lord of the Church. Confidence in that truth is the seed-bed of growth.

Warmth and enthusiasm
The second thing a fire does is to warm the house and make it inviting. How does this apply to the life of the Church? I mentioned at the start of this address that around the fire Joseph and Mary and their children would have gathered for fun and fellowship. As a matter of fact, from the physical realities of heat and cold have come many of our everyday analogies. We talk of being 'cold as ice', 'hot blooded', 'cold blooded', 'on fire', and so on.

When the fire of the Holy Spirit falls, he warms our hearts for the things of God. In a word, he *enthuses* us. The word enthusiasm comes from a root meaning 'God-intoxicated'. Sadly, in some parishes I find more apathy than enthusiasm. Enthusiasm usually leads to growth, when coupled with sensitivity and knowledge. Apathy, whatever it is linked with, declines into death. I love the opening words of the Magnificat: 'My soul magnifies the Lord, and my spirit rejoices in God my Saviour' (Luke 1.46-47). Mary's heart was enlarged with a great vision of God who comes to overthrow the oppressor and rescue the poor. Service begins with praise. You priests –

let your service for Christ arise from the warmth of your praise. You fellow Christians – never lose the warm love for your Lord, because that is the very centre of your service for him.

I'd love to see the warmth and enthusiasm of the Spirit spilling over into our worship on Sundays. Yes, let there be dignity, colour, light and majesty in our worship. Yes, let there be solemnity and reverence at the high points of our celebration. Does that have to mean coldness, reserve and a frowning aloofness that drives ordinary people away? Of course not! These characteristics have no real place in vibrant Christian worship, whether of Catholic or Evangelical variety. Let us have warmth as well as dignity, smiles alongside the serious, and joy at the heart of it all.

Power and conviction
Finally, there is something about fire when it is small and controllable that is lovely, but uncontrolled it is unpredictable and rather frightening. Think of the might of a forest fire or the burning heat of the sun.

There is, we have to say, something unpredictable about the work of the Holy Spirit. Mary was to find that out as time went on. She was sent out on an adventure which took her from the Annunciation to Pentecost, and the questions and uncertainties built up. There were times when the ministry of her Son left her feeling cut out of the action, and she was amazed and perhaps frightened at what she had unleashed on the world. The questions led up to the cross and even beyond it. On that cross her dying Son said to John: 'Behold, your mother!' (John 19.27) There she lost everything that really mattered. Surely there could not have been a more destructive fire than Calvary; but more was to come. Through the resurrection the fire scorched forth at Pentecost and to the foundation of the Church. The fire, burning its way through the structures of old Israel, created a new community of faith and love.

I would like to enlarge on this theme, but I dare not because our experience falls far short of what we dimly perceive in the pages of Scripture. Much as we love our Church, we know it falls far short of its inheritance of faith. Listen to Alec Vidler:

A great book, a bell-ringing book about the Holy Spirit could be written, though it might be in the form of a poem or a novel rather than a theological treatise. The reason why this book has not yet been written is that conscious experience of the presence and life of the Spirit among contemporary Christians is so thin and weak and hampered that conditions do not exist in which anyone can write with full-blooded conviction on the subject.
(*Christian Belief*, SCM 1957).

How may we change those conditions so that the book may be written, or, more importantly, that lives may be changed through that same Spirit of power? We know that 'theologically' only he can do it, but we can play our part. I dream, I hope and I pray that in our diocese we shall see God's Spirit, the Spirit that fell on Mary, coming to us and doing great things for God. Won't it be wonderful when it happens that you and I will be able to share a little secret that, in the womb of Walsingham, on our diocesan retreat, a prayer was uttered and a commitment determined. There in 1988 a little vision of God was seen; there we were strengthened by the Spirit of God to go back to our deaneries and parishes more confident, more convinced of the truths of our faith, to share him with others in the way that Mary did.

PART THREE:
THE CHURCH'S YEAR

12

Advent: 'Now is the Acceptable Time'
Mark Parish Church, Advent Sunday, 3 December 1990

Quite a few years ago now I was at a Family Service on an Advent Sunday, and the young curate began his talk with a question addressed to the children. 'Can anyone tell me', he asked, 'what is the special name for today?'

The answer given by one little boy will always remain with me. 'Sir,' he said, 'today is Adventure Sunday.' What a good answer! Of course, that is what Advent is all about – God's adventure in breaking into our history and making it 'his-story'.

What does Advent mean for us today? How can we make sense of it? Let me first introduce you to my text: 2 Corinthians 6.2. 'Now is the acceptable time; behold, now is the day of salvation.'

In this passage Paul, writing quite soon after the death and resurrection of Jesus Christ, is quite emphatic in stating that, because of Jesus Christ, God's time has invaded ours, and this is the moment of decision.

Advent reminds us of the significance of God's time. I wonder if you are aware that in the Bible there are two words for time and that, generally speaking, they refer to two quite different ideas. The first word is used to describe ordinary time – past, present and future. The word used is *chronos*, from which comes our word 'chronology'. So dates like 1066 or Aunt Ethel's birthday all belong to *chronos* time.

The other word, *kairos*, is a word that is used a great deal to describe God's breaking into our time and history to bring his salvation. Through Christ, God has made sense of time, and the moment of his 'breaking in' becomes the moment of discovery, hope and salvation. It was with this meaning in mind that Paul told his readers: 'Now is the acceptable time *(kairos)*;

behold, now is the day of salvation.'

In a limited way we can understand this, because for all of us certain dates stand out with striking significance. Let me ask some members of the congregation a few questions:

First, the Vicar: Why is 12 August special for you? Reply: It's the anniversary of my wedding.

To Susan: Why is 12 December a day you will never forget? Reply: It was the day my child was born.

To Andy: 12 July is important to you. Why? Reply: It was the day I passed my exam.

Days like that are very important to us. We measure happiness and sadness by momentous things that happened on occasions such as these. A day passes from being merely ordinary *(chronos)* into one irradiated with a special significance *(kairos)* because of the event with which it is permanently associated.

Let me give you another example. I still recall the day John Kennedy died. I was sitting on the top deck of a London bus when the news travelled from passenger to passenger: 'The President of the United States has been shot.' The bus pulled over to the side of the road and the driver rushed into a newsagent's shop to get the facts. It was terrible news. This was not the shooting of an ordinary man, but that of the President of the United States. We were all caught up in the shock and wondered what the significance was.

For the Christian, God's time is Jesus-time: his coming. By his coming to us as a human being and by his suffering, dying and rising for us, our lives have meaning and hope. *Kairos* time has invaded *chronos* time.

This takes me into my second point: *Advent means that through Christ this world has a destiny because God has poured into it his hope.* As we approach Christmas the real tragedy is that the vast majority of our friends – good, sincere people, most of them – will not get within a mile of the real meaning of Christmas. There will be rejoicing – but at what? There will be feasting – but for what? There will be drinking and revelling – but to what end? Our friends will still be thinking of Christmas as *chronos* time – just another festival.

The German philosopher Ernst Bloch, who incidentally was a communist, once analysed modern society as suffering from a disease he called 'death by bread alone'. He wrote: 'It is like a vast supermarket in which absentmindedly, yet intent on what we are doing, we push our shopping trolleys up one aisle and down the other, while death and alienation have the run of the place.' This 'death by bread alone' concept means that people in the West have lost sight of spiritual and eternal values and now only perceive material and temporal aims. We are like Hans Christian Anderson's tale of the Emperor who believed he was clothed in the finest garments – but all the time he was naked.

For the Christian who is living in the shadow of Advent, this life is no longer a 'cul-de-sac' but a road of hope, because God has taken up residence here. Gerard Manley Hopkins' great poem 'God's Grandeur' puts it so well:

The world is charged with the grandeur of God.
    It will flame out, like shining from shook foil; . . .

Hopkins goes on:

And for all this, nature is never spent;
    There lives the dearest freshness deep down things;

The Christian agrees. We look at life, we look at the values that Christ has introduced, we look at the unity between the worlds of spirit and matter and we are in no doubt that we abide in God's eternal love. 'There lives the dearest freshness deep down things.'

Advent signals values: that God loved us so much that he was willing to enter upon an adventure that cost him the death of his Son. That love continues, and one day will be the reason for his coming as Saviour and, yes, as Judge.

What is our response? Let me give you two quite different answers. The first, alas, is all too common. It is told by Tony Hancock in 'The Blood Donor', a classic episode in his wonderful TV series. In it he boasts of his gifts to charity, all written down in his little black book:

Half a crown to Arab refugees, one shilling and three-pence for the lifeboats, sixpence to Christian Aid, five bob to Help the Aged, self-denial week – ninepence. When the great Audit Day comes and the Great Accountant says to me, 'And what did you do?', I shall hand him my little black book and say, "Ere you are, Mate. Add that little lot up!'

It's a good story but the ending is wrong, because you and I have nothing to contribute except our brokenness, our help-lessness and weakness. The story speaks as though the Great Auditor is a total stranger.

A far better story and, dare I say it, a more Christian under-standing, comes from my second illustration. It happened to me in Watford many years ago. I was returning from a hospital where I had been visiting someone, and I was last in a bus queue. It was a very foggy evening and extremely cold. The other people in the queue had obviously been waiting longer than I and were moaning and groaning. The bus was so late. Then we heard the sound of a vehicle. Excitement changed to despair as people realized it wasn't the bus – only a car, which crawled past us. Suddenly it stopped, and reversed until it was level with me. Out of the fog came a voice: 'George? George Carey? Is that you?' I recognized the voice! It was a close friend. Thankfully I accepted his invitation to 'jump in the back', and home we sped.

Let's continue the story for just a moment in a ridiculous way. Let us imagine that, back at the bus stop, the other people were furious. 'What right had he to accept that lift?' cries one lady. 'I was in the queue before him. It's not fair!' But it was fair. You see, she did not know the driver. I did. That made all the difference.

The story, I believe, goes to the heart of what Advent is all about. It is about a relationship that changes the way we look at life; it is about a friendship that will take us through life, facing the black moments as well as the good; it is about God's time breaking into our lives, giving them hope and meaning and joy.

'Now is the acceptable time; behold, now . . .'

13

Christmas: A Sign of God with Us
Wells Cathedral, Christmas 1988

In December 1859 the editorial of a leading scientific journal concluded its survey of scientific achievements with the statement: 'No significant piece of research or outstanding discovery happened this year.' What an academic gaffe – that was the year that saw the publication of Charles Darwin's *The Origin of Species*, a book that was to shake the very foundations of Western thought!

In a similar way, a Roman soldier writing from Palestine to his parents in about 4 BC might well have written: 'This is an out-of-the-way dump. Fancy getting posted to this land of war-crazy illiterates.' And yet, that land of 'war-crazy illiterates' was to be the birthplace of Jesus Christ: the person whose words and actions have inspired millions of people down the centuries.

Christmas is for most of us a magical moment in the year when we gather with our families, sing familiar carols and see the delight in the eyes of the children as they open their stockings and presents. But what makes it most special for the Christian is the celebration of the coming of God's Son into our troubled world.

There can be no disputing the word 'troubled' either. We celebrate this Christmas in the shadow of three awful human tragedies – the earthquake in Armenia in the Soviet Union; the train crash in north London and now, this week, the air disaster in Lockerbie. How dreadful. It could also be that for some of you 1988 has also seen some trouble, a bereavement perhaps, that has shaken you to the foundations. You will be wondering, what is the message of Christmas for me this year in the face of this or that problem? Listen then to the message of the angel in Luke 2.10,12: 'I bring you good news of a great joy which will come to all the people . . . And this will be a sign for you: you will find a babe wrapped in swaddling cloths and lying in a manger.'

A *sign* – and it is important to remember that Christmas itself is only a sign. A sign speaks of something beyond itself. All the trappings of Christmas – the decorated tree, lights, the presents we give, the crib, tinsel, crackers, the eating and drinking which make up our celebrations – are only 'signs'. The sign or the symbol, however, can be ignored and treated as an end in itself. For many people, Christmas is a time to have an apocalyptic hangover or binge; the Christian bit is an unnecessary encumbrance to them. For others, Christmas is a welcome relief from the pressure of work and a time to recuperate. For busy housewives, Christmas can present itself with other problems – over-excited children and a million and one things to do. Little wonder then that at this festive season of good will to all people, arguments and friction mock our pretence at peace and sometimes split the family.

So, we have to ask again: What, please, is Christmas a sign of?

It is a sign of God's presence with us.

You see, even at the time it was only a sign. The baby did not open its eyes and start preaching a sermon. He did not hand out sayings of Jesus in a little red book, or give them Christmas presents. The baby was only a sign and could only have been understood later in the light of the life of the person who was to be the Saviour of the world. Indeed, here is a reminder that Christmas can only be understood in the light of later events, can only be discovered in all its wonderful freshness and life when we discover for ourselves that Jesus is the human face of God.

We also discover at this point the reality of love at the heart of the sign. Just think for a moment of the way love is expressed in our giving. All right, I know that one of us will get the inevitable bottle of aftershave, or talcum powder. There was a time when I could have stocked a chemist's shop with male toiletries! Yet leaving that aside, our gifts are signs of our love or respect for one another. Parents know what their children are longing for and will give them what they want, even if every piggy bank in the house has to be broken open. Love gives. You see, there are many talkers about: politicians who want to change society but have not got time to help their next door neighbour; Christians who want to sing their hymns but can't be bothered to get involved in their local church. It is not love if it is locked up in the vaults of our dreams for a better world and a happier life. Love has to move from idea to reality, and that is always God's way – the way of incarnation. That theological word is a wonderful word describing God's action of becoming human for each one of us. No faith is more materialistic than God's surprising action of sending Jesus into our world for us.

In one of his books, David Jenkins speaks of a cartoon which shows God sitting on a cloud looking very cross and saying: 'You love one another or I'll come down there and thump you.'

Well, he does come down – not to thump us but to love us in Jesus, to teach us the Christian way, and to take our sins and failures to the cross and to rise again in triumph for us all.

A sign of God with us.

But a sign also of God's commitment to his world.

You see, Christmas is linked with the season of Advent – the season of hope which sets before us the hope of his coming to restore all things and bring all things to a glorious conclusion. So the angels sang the *Gloria*: 'Glory to God in the highest, and on earth peace among men with whom he is pleased!' (Luke 2.14)

Yes, we grieve when tragedy strikes in such awful forms as we have seen recently. We are heartbroken when death comes in its ugly presence into our homes, and we dislike the unpalatable fact of impermanence. But the message of Christmas is that God will never leave us and his love will endure for ever, which makes Christmas a real celebration of God's commitment to our world and makes sense of all our hopes and dreams.

This can only be fully understood, however, when we as individuals make our own personal and spiritual visit to Bethlehem. You may know the delightful story of G.K. Chesterton who was always getting lost. One day he found himself at Market Harborough but with no idea where he was going. So he sent a telegram to his wife saying: 'Am in Market Harborough – where ought I to be?' and she, being a practical woman, sent a terse telegram with one word: 'Home'.

That is the message of Christmas: come home. Come home to his love. Come home to an understanding of the world which puts God back at the centre of it. Christmas is not the reality of the Christian faith: it is a sign of God's gracious invitation to celebrate his love personally by welcoming him into our hearts and lives, not just once a year but every day we live. In the words of the poem by Angelus Silesius:

Tho' Christ a thousand times in Bethlehem is born
If he's not born in thee, thou art still forlorn.

May God bless us all this Christmas time as we make our way to the manger and celebrate the gift of his love and life.

14

The Epiphany: Strangers Discover Christ

The Bishop's farewell address to the Cathedral of Bath and
Wells, Epiphany Sunday, 6 January 1991

I am going to talk about the familiar and rich story of the visit of the Magi, the wise men, to the infant Christ, from Matthew 2.1-12. Epiphany is one of the oldest festivals in the Church, far older than Christmas. It introduces a wonderful idea, that strangers from afar find the Christ and discover him to be the Saviour of the world. Let me mention three things very briefly this morning.

A puzzling question

'Where is he who has been born king of the Jews?' (Matthew 2.2) This is an ancient question, but as up to date as the latest computer. Of course, we might put it a different way today: 'Can God be known, and is the Christian faith the answer to human needs?' This, I want to submit, is far more important than many of the material questions and issues that fill our waking hours – questions of food, jobs, ambition and human happiness. If God *is*, then it makes all these other things worthwhile. In other words, if in Jesus Christ I find the answer to the question 'Where is he?' then all the transitory questions of life find genuine meaning around this wonderful centre.

So we find these men – were they three in number? Who knows? – making a long journey. I saw on a church bill-board recently the familiar statement, 'Wise men still seek Christ'. They do, and it is still a quest worth becoming a question: 'Where is he?' The firm answer given by the Christian faith is, look no further than Jesus Christ. He can meet the longings of the human heart. Go to him, abide in him, trust in him, look to him.

Some of you may have heard me say before that when I was

a young ordinand I met up with a marvellous Canadian bishop, Ralph Dean. There he stood in the college chapel, grizzled and weather-beaten by harsh Canadian winters. He came out with a wonderful phrase which has stayed with me over the years. 'If you feel that God is far, far away, remember this – he has not moved.'

A peculiar place

God pops up in the most surprising of places. Fancy him turning up in a snivelling little place like Bethlehem. Of course, today it has romantic overtones. Go to Bethlehem today, and in spite of the unrest there, it has that undeniable atmosphere of prayer and sanctity poured into it by millions of pilgrims and visitors. What a holy place – but only insofar as in that place the Saviour became a human person and started his adventure of faith. Bethlehem means 'house of bread', and the One born there became the 'bread of life' who becomes our spiritual food today. Yet Bethlehem the place is no more special, really, than any other place now: because the coming of Christ into our world has sanctified every place, every place becomes holy, where he may be found: your homes, your places of work, and, yes, in a special way, churches like this glorious Cathedral of Wells.

Sometimes bishops get ridiculous letters. I received a few not so long ago complaining about this place, saying that it does not speak of God; that it is a monument to a man-made religion; that it ought to be pulled down and a block of flats built here instead, and the money spent on missionary work abroad. Well, the Dean and I took great joy in disabusing that person of that mistaken view. Indeed, not so long ago I received another letter from an American woman who came to Wells two years ago. Her marriage was in ruins but here in this place she found peace. She prayed here and thought about her marriage; she vowed to do something about it. She lit a candle over there as a silent prayer for her estranged husband and went home. She wrote to me saying that in this place she found it possible to forgive for the first time and then return home to seek reconciliation. It is my desire that this lovely place, made valid with all the prayers and hopes of generations of worshippers, will continue to be open, friendly, worshipful, adaptable and meaningful to us all.

A hazardous journey

The Magi had found the answer to their question in a simple child and, in T.S. Eliot's words: 'no longer at home in the old dispensation', they returned home having found and having been found. No doubt the journey back was as hazardous as it was coming. That is also a parable of life. We cannot say that having faith in Christ makes life easy. Of course not. Faith is always an adventure of trust and hope. It is not an easy, cost-free ride, but it is the constant working out of our hopes and fears. For myself and Eileen as we move on to a ministry which will have its own surprises in the days ahead, we hope that we can lead our beloved Church on. In spite of the obvious gains in recent years – and no one could be more grateful than I to Robert Runcie and all he achieved – we now need a period of calmness, of peace, to grow and get on with the real work of caring for others and serving Christ in and through others. The real work of the Church is not done, as anyone in his or her sane mind knows, at General Synod. The real work of the Church is done in every ordinary place of worship.

You and I have this wonderful mission to share Christ with others, this mysterious treasure who alone can make sense of it all. I love the rabbinic story of Rabbi Schmelke who lived in Russia. One day a very poor man came begging at his door. 'I have nothing and I have five children to feed,' he pleaded. Now Rabbi Schmelke and his wife were as poor as the beggar. But the rabbi was a very kind man and his heart went out to the poor man. He remembered that his wife had one precious jewel, and he did what no man should ever do – he went and gave his wife's only jewel to the beggar. No sooner had he shut the door than his wife found him out. 'But that was a very precious jewel!' she stormed. So the rabbi ran after the man and said: 'I have just found out that the jewel I gave you is more precious than I thought – don't sell it for too little.' I think there is a parable in that for you and me as we seek to share Christ today.

15

Lent: The Glory of the Cross

Five talks given in Wells Cathedral during Lent,
March-April 1988

In these addresses we are going to contemplate the cross of
Jesus from five different angles. We will consider its mystery
as well as its glory.

Before we begin, we need to take on board the mystery, a
word which will follow us through the five sessions. I do not
claim to be able to unravel the complexities of atonement. If I
am able to offer a small flicker of light, that will give me great
joy! The cross is a mystery. Indeed, I will go further. In the
New Testament period it was obviously an embarrassment.
For the Romans, crucifixion was a penalty reserved for criminals and for outcasts. For the first Christians to claim this as
the heart of their faith was a scandal of the first order.

Now it has to be said that the people of that period could at
least understand such notions as 'sacrifice', 'propitiation' and
'atonement'. For us that entire world-view has disappeared.
We are not used to such notions and there are few world
religions that still offer 'sacrifices'. We do not believe that it is
necessary to placate God in such a way. Indeed, it may be
argued that the success of Christianity in establishing the
finality of the cross in dealing with sin 'once and for all' has
removed from our minds its roots in the common experience
of our lives. So our problem is understanding *why* it should
have ever occurred to God that we needed redeeming, saving,
restoring, in such a radical way. *Why* was it necessary? *Why*
couldn't God let bygones be bygones? *Why* did God choose
that particular form?

Not all the notions concerning sacrifice are entirely absent
from our lives. We speak of the 'sacrifices' we make for one
another – that notion rings many bells. We speak of a mother

sacrificing her life for her children. We are used to evil men demanding a ransom before their victim can be released. Terry Waite languishes in Lebanon – but it is possible to believe that if our Government came up with a suitably attractive offer, he would be released. So the ideas are still very meaningful in our world, but what we are saying about the cross is this: *that in this particular way and through this particular person, God chose to redeem humankind. It was final, it was full and it was free.*

Let us distinguish between the two words 'atonement' and 'salvation': atonement refers to a past event, but salvation speaks of it continuing into the future. We might like to have that distinction in mind as these lectures continue. The problem is clear. Christians claim that what happened on Good Friday was decisive for humankind – it was of such a definitive, absolute nature that it split world history in two and it declares that the many strands of human experience (hope, joy, peace, human fulfilment) run through the crossroads of the cross. That is quite a claim!

I am now going to offer you five ways of interpreting the cross. Towards the end of each I will describe a recent example of a person who lived and suffered in such a way.

I. Jesus – Our Example

In 1 Peter 2, the writer looks at Jesus from the viewpoint of suffering Christians and says: 'Yes, I know all that you are enduring . . . look at Jesus . . . follow him.' It was certainly the case that in the first centuries the example of Jesus must have been a tremendous model for living and for dying. Consider Jesus; keep him before you as your icon. He suffered for you, so suffer for him.

In life, no doubt all of us have been inspired by the example of others – parents, teachers, friends. Sometimes it has been a case of seeing something done really well and it inspires us to do it even better. An artist friend once remarked: 'I saw this chap make something out of an ordinary piece of wood – he fashioned it into an exquisite work of art.' He was so inspired that he became an artist too.

Yet the idea of Jesus as our example did not become a theory of atonement until the twelfth and thirteenth centuries, and I want to introduce you now to our first theologian – Peter Abelard. That particular period of history saw the rise of some wonderful thinkers – Bernard of Clairvaux, Thomas à Kempis, Meister Eckhart. It was an age dominated by new ideas, new discoveries and particularly by mysticism based on love.

Peter Abelard himself was a fascinating and unusual man. Some of you may have read the book by Helen Waddell about him and his love for Héloïse. Peter was a monk, a scholar with a brilliant, innovative mind. There was a tragic, brief love affair which was doomed to fail, and it is not our concern here. What is our concern, though, is the notion of love which he saw was at the centre of understanding the work of Christ. He had inherited a view of the cross which saw it as the place where Christ did something which changed God's mind about human beings. It satisfied God's honour – a price had to be paid and Christ paid it. The analogies at the time were very crude and based upon feudal understandings of barons and servants and themes of honour, respect and dignity. Peter Abelard rejected these crude and often absurd ideas which seemed to lower the dignity of God. In their place he sub-stituted a psychological theory which is almost modern in its understanding and penetration. He saw the power of love to inspire and transform. In his opinion, the cross of Christ did not change God, or *our relationship* with God at all, but it changes us. The cross does not affect God because he has always been loving and desiring our repentance; it affects us by presenting us with an example of love and sacrifice which overwhelms us because of its outrageous generosity.

Let us now dig a little deeper into this theory and try to appreciate Abelard's thought from within. For him the power of love is paramount. For Abelard there is a transforming energy in love which can change people. Perhaps that came from his own experience of human love – we don't really know. We have all seen love change things. Look what the love of another human being does to human behaviour. Look at what the love of literature, art, sport, does to people's attitudes and patterns of life. For Abelard, then, the cross was an act of love which, though past, still has immense capacity to create. Listen to him writing to Héloïse about the power of the story of love:

Put yourself in the position of one of the bystanders on
the path of Christ's passion: Are you not moved to tears
of remorse by the only Begotten Son of God, who for you
and all mankind, in his innocence, was seized, dragged
along, blindfolded, mocked, spat upon, crowned with
thorns, finally hanged between thieves on the cross? . . .
Keep him in mind. Look at him going to be crucified for
your sake. Be one of the crowd, one of the women who
wept and lamented over him . . . In your mind be always
present at his tomb, weep and wail with the faithful
women . . . Prepare with them the perfumes for his burial.

Let me now mention two particular ideas in Abelard's theory of the power of love. First, the one I have already drawn
attention to – love is *infused in us* by revealing love. The cross,
in his view, is like a gigantic visual aid which shocks, horrifies
and draws our pity and our concern. So, Abelard says, consider, look, keep him in mind.

Second, Abelard concentrates upon the action of salvation.
He does not narrowly concentrate on the last week of Jesus'
life; the entire life of Jesus was an example of sacrificial love.
Christ 'illuminates' us by his teaching, by his prayer life and
all the deeds of his incarnation. The death of Jesus was its
tremendous climax.

So what do you and I make of this theory? Does it not make
a lot of sense because it rings true to our experience? Love has
that effect on us. But this theory, which is sometimes called
'the moral influence' theory, is considered to have a number
of weaknesses that we should look at.

First, does it underestimate the power of sinfulness in us
all? Let me give some very basic illustrations. Suppose I am a
very heavy smoker and I am anxious to break the habit, and
you say to me: 'What a wonderful man is the Bishop of Bristol;
he never smoked a cigarette in his life. Make him your
example. Consider him.' Suppose you are on drugs and you
know what they are doing to your body but you can't break
the habit. You are a slave, you are weak and it is no good for
someone to say to you, 'Just follow my example', because at
moments like that the intrinsic goodness of another person
becomes an impossible dream. They are who they are, and I
am who I am – the gulf appears unbridgeable. The example

may be inspiring, but I need a new 'me' to get to where I want to go. So Abelard's theory seems to present me with a challenge as formidable as climbing Mount Everest.

Some thinkers have gone further and have even said that Abelard's idea of sin is superficial and inadequate. Perhaps it is. Experience of life suggests that evil does ravage our capacity to listen to God and hear him; it does lead to deterioration of character and to further separation from God. If people are unwilling to consider the suffering of Christ, how can it ever have power to change them? The theory seems then rather intellectual and remote from everyday experience.

A second criticism is that the theory assumes that all emotional response is the same. Dr Kenneth Kirk offered this criticism years ago, that some people are moved more easily than others by suffering and death. There are emotional types and there are some who are matter-of-fact and fairly cold in their emotional response. This idea does leave out in the cold some of us who are not moved that much by emotion. Then there is another point that I have just touched upon: if sin degrades and hardens us, then this will affect our emotional response anyway and make it even harder for the cross to be effective in inspiring us to change our way of living.

Third, it has been argued that Abelard's theory is too subjective. We have already seen that it rejects any notion that God is changed. For this reason the theory has been called a subjective theory of atonement because it insists that the cross changes us, not God; that he is always forgiving. Does not this make forgiveness cheap grace and God himself a rather indulgent parent who is never put out by anything we do? If it is true that humankind is fallen, that we are separated from the presence of God by our failure and helplessness and are in need of God's forgiveness, Abelard's views do not reflect sufficiently well the seriousness of our predicament. They make it all too easy and cheap.

Yet Abelard's theory cannot be rejected totally. It has to start with other ideas, offering us a clue or two as to why God chose this particular route for his Son and for us. Let me pick out three aspects that may help to guide us.

The way of love. When we look at the cross it does tell us how much God loves us. Love is only fully understood by what it does. We only really know love when it is expressed in action;

when people demonstrate it. Do you recall the story of Jesus at the house of Simon the Pharisee? A woman came and poured ointment over his feet. When Simon despised Jesus in his heart, Jesus replied: 'Her sins, which are many, are forgiven, for she loved much; but he who is forgiven little, loves little' (Luke 7.47). Her love showed in what she gave.

In what way is the life and death of Jesus an example of God's love? This is the Achilles' heel of Abelard's theory, because Christ's death is only explicable if it saves us from a serious and dreadful predicament which is of eternal significance. Christ's example is not that of helping us across a road, or showing us what good neighbours we must be – but costly, redemptive, self-emptying love; love which lays down its life for others so that they might be restored to God.

The way of sacrifice. Love and sacrifice, of course, belong together because love is never wholly platonic. Love is a sacrifice that comes in the willingness to be emptied out in selfless giving. The sacrifice comes in dying for that valued person or thing. Yet, for love, it is never called or named sacrifice. Any parent knows that. We pour much time, money, anxiety and effort into our children simply for the pleasure of seeing them grow into the kind of people we long for them to be. Yet it is sacrifice which is offered in delight. We only start to talk about sacrifice with our children when something seriously wrong has happened in the relationship, when the mother or father says bitterly: 'Don't you understand what I have given up for you? My career, my ambition, my dreams – and all that does not mean a fig to you!'

The way of understanding. Human love can also be misunderstood. We sometimes ask about a person: 'Why has she chosen that course of action? What on earth do they see in one another? Why has he thrown up that promising career in politics to become a vicar?' The point about love is its unpredictability; it has the capacity to surprise and even scandalize. So it was with Jesus: he scandalized people by the company he kept, by the overturning of values which had become the cement of his society but which he saw as being barriers for people. He chose a way of loving which was so outrageous and costly that only a few friends could follow him into his dark night of the soul.

Let me now illustrate some of these things by introducing you to a twentieth-century saint who lived a life of love in a radical way. Her name was Lisa Skobtsova, and she was born in Riga in 1891, and studied in Russia. Her father's death when she was eighteen destroyed her faith. How could she believe in God in such a world as this? 'There is no God, only sorrow, wickedness and injustice in the world.' She poured herself into self-sacrifice now for another cause – the People. She married another student and together they joined the communist party. Lisa was a close friend of Tolstoy and Berdyaev but rejected their Christian ideas. She joined a plot to assassinate Trotsky and had to flee to France. In exile she expected their first child, having left her husband in Russia; he was later killed, and she suffered the blow of another death – her own child. Yet this death led her back to God and restored her faith. She found Christian friends and found a Cause more wonderful to die for. Her great ability was to get through to the outcasts of society – the drunks, the crazed, the depressed. She would go into seamy dives, sitting there, listening, consoling. Orthodox Christian eyebrows were raised. How could she go around with such undesirables?

In 1932 she became a nun and was given the name Maria 'in memory of St Maria of Egypt who lived a life of penitence in the desert'. Maria saw her mission to go out to act and speak in the desert of human hearts. For her, the life of a conventional nun, a safe and comfortable existence separate from the misery and filth of the world was just not possible. That was not the example of the Lord. The war came, she was swept up with many others by the Germans and ended up in Ravensbrück concentration camp. There she served others sacrificially. She was given the chance to leave the camp on a number of occasions, but she waived the right so that others might go. She died on Easter Eve, 1945. The following day, Easter Day, the Red Cross entered the camp. Maria followed Christ to the end; he was her inspiring Lord, he had changed her life and she knew he could change others. Her job was to live the cross.

Let me give a brief application. Abelard's theory, coming out of the experiences and theology of his day, presents a challenge to modern Christians who, all too easily, over-intellectualize their faith. Abelard encourages us to see the cross as a moving force for change. Perhaps this is a challenge to put it at the centre of our lives, to think about it and, this Lent, to read the story as if we were there. Perhaps it is a challenge to our Church to be a more cross-oriented fellowship, living it, and working out what it means.

II. Jesus – Our Pioneer

If there is a hymn that encapsulates the example theory embraced by Peter Abelard it must be that well-known verse from C.F. Alexander's hymn, 'There is a green hill far away':

> O dearly, dearly has he loved,
> And we must love him too,
> And trust in his redeeming blood,
> And try his works to do.

Of course, Alexander would not in the slightest deny the more traditional view. You will remember she wrote:

> There was no other good enough
> To pay the price of sin;
> He only could unlock the gate
> Of heaven, and let us in.

In this second talk I want to mention a view which has a long history in the Church, far longer than my previous subject. I call the subject 'Jesus – our Pioneer' because that seems to sum up the thrust of the idea. The word 'pioneer' only occurs three times in the New Testament and the most important occurrence is found in Hebrews 12.2.

The idea of a pioneer was a very important one for the early Christians. They were aware that in a deep way Jesus had dealt a death blow to sin and death, but they believed there was more to it than that. They saw him also as a trail- blazer, someone who goes ahead of others and prepares the way. Neil Armstrong is a good example, as the first man to walk on the moon: 'One small step for man, one giant leap for mankind.' We might think of a pioneer as someone who goes into the wilderness to prepare a home for others.

The first theologian I want to introduce you to now is a

second-century Christian called Irenaeus.

Irenaeus was bishop of a tiny Christian community in Lyons towards the end of the second century. The Christians faced fierce persecution and opposition, especially from a more numerous religious group known as the Gnostics. This group's theory of salvation attempted to incorporate Christ into their concept of God, but it was at a formidable price – he was just one of a number of divine beings in the pantheon.

Against this, Irenaeus asserted the primacy of Jesus for God's plan of salvation and, in opposition to a formidable heresy, developed the first Christian theology outside of the New Testament. Irenaeus begins with Adam. In his view Adam was not a fully developed being when he transgressed God's Law. He was young and vulnerable and was thus easy prey for the wiles of the Evil One. A key passage of Scripture for Irenaeus was Ephesians 1, where God's plan for human-kind is mentioned. Irenaeus saw a key word in this – *anakepha-laiosis* – which in the English translation means 'to unite all things'. However, the word can equally be translated 'to reca-pitulate', meaning that Christ summed up all things in him-self. There is a line from a familiar hymn which captures this idea very well: 'A second Adam to the fight and to the rescue came.' We can easily see what Irenaeus was exploring. Adam and Eve were created by God for a glorious destiny with him. They were not fully developed human beings; they had just begun. The Evil One saw his chance and robbed them of their destiny. The second Adam came, however, not only to save humankind, but to take us on to the destiny that should have been ours in the first place. We can see then that Irenaeus's idea was very optimistic. Christ recapitulated all of Adam's sin and restored us to God. Indeed, God made of it something more wonderful than anybody could have thought. There is a snatch of this in the Roman Mass for Easter Day which talks in terms of '*O felix culpa*' – 'O blessed sin which wrought man's redemption'. Without the sin of Adam we would have been deprived of the wonder of our salvation.

A second element in this theory is that Jesus entered into every aspect of human life and sanctifies it with his presence and love. I must confess that I find this deeply attractive, and I want to draw attention to a few Bible passages where I think this idea is being worked out. We see it, for example, in the

birth of Jesus. Of course the infancy narratives stress the
divinity of Christ, but they are also emphasizing the incarnation of Christ as he shares our nature in his human growth and
development. We see him depicted as a young boy in Luke 2,
obedient to his parents, going up to the Temple and spending
time with the learned men asking questions. Hebrews 5.8-9
tells us that: 'Although he was a Son, he learned obedience
through what he suffered; and being made perfect he became
the source of eternal salvation to all who obey him.'

Why do I find that attractive?

I am suspicious of gods who dwell benignly in heavens,
immutable and supreme. Here is a Messiah who by becoming
one of us knows all about human weakness, about human life
and development. He knows all about sadness, temptation
and the grubby facts of life. I can take comfort in this, knowing
that my Lord has entered into our humanity and brought it
home to God. You see, this view takes incarnation seriously.
It is so easy for Western Protestantism to fall into the trap of
thinking that the last week of Jesus' life is all-important. Well,
it is important. Without it there would be no Christianity! But
all that preceded it was very important too. We must never
separate incarnation and atonement. The whole of Christ's life
was atoning. He entered deeply into our pain and grief. 'Surely he has borne our griefs and carried our sorrows', says Isaiah
53.4.

Let me go on now and tease out three aspects of this
'pioneer' idea.

Jesus our pioneer overcomes death. Hebrews 2 contains a fascinating idea that Jesus had to be made human in order to
overcome death for us; that is to say, he pioneered our way
through the deep waters of death. In Hebrews 2.9 we read:
'But we see Jesus, who for a little while was made lower than
the angels, crowned with glory and honour because of the
suffering of death, so that by the grace of God he might taste
death for every one.'

Jesus became a trail-blazer through the darkness of death
and overcame it. This is a familiar idea in the New Testament.
The New Testament writers were in no doubt that Jesus,
through his resurrection, dealt a mortal blow to death and
freed us from its influence and power. Most of us will remember John Donne's wonderful lines:

Death, be not proud, though some have callèd thee
Mighty and dreadful, for thou art not so,
For those whom thou think'st thou dost overthrow
Die not, poor Death; nor yet canst thou kill me . . .
                    Why swell'st thou then?
One short sleep past, we wake eternally,
And Death shall be no more: Death, thou shalt die!

It is a wonderful comfort to know that Jesus has entered into
our dying and will deliver us from it. Fear of dying still grips
our hearts. Perhaps some of us here tonight are still gripped
by fear of death. One person said to me a year or two ago: 'I'm
scared of dying. Yes, I believe in Jesus, but sometimes I wake
up in the night just petrified.'

Let us face up to the reality of these fears and face them in
the power of the cross.

Jesus our pioneer overcomes apparent failure. Let's go back to
the Greek idea of Jesus entering into our sinfulness and weakness. If you ever get the chance of going to the catacombs in
Rome you will see on the walls a very popular image of the
cross shaped as an anchor. Sometimes the anchor will be
fashioned as a fish-hook. The fish-hook image had an interesting story behind it. Some of the later Greek thinkers developed Irenaeus's idea of Jesus defeating the power of evil,
and they created a very vivid image of the defeat of Satan. The
picture was that of Christ impaled on a cross shaped like a
fish-hook. Satan, visualized as a great fish seeing his enemy
in such distress, swoops to devour but gets more than he
bargains for. He is hooked.

We can quickly dispense with the crude mythology, but I
like the concept of apparent failure. It is clear that in the eyes
of Jesus' contemporaries the cross was a contemptuous symbol. Indeed, the cross was such an enormous stumbling block
that we have in it a rather surprising proof of the genuineness
of primitive Christianity. If you were going to invent a brand
new religion you would not start with a cross. The cross
denoted that the mission of Jesus had failed. It was over. The
resurrection is God's vindication of the apparent failure.

I want to suggest to you that God has a far more positive
attitude to failure than most of us. We don't like failing; it
hurts our pride; it brings us down to the dust. God, however,

sees the opportunity to recreate something new out of the failure we see. Some years ago I saw on TV a most splendid series by a marvellous writer called Brian Clark. Called 'The Late Starter', it is the story of a retired professor, Edward Brett. Unknown to him, his wife is a gambler, who over the years has been secretly gambling away his money and assets. The discovery is made on the day he retires. He returns home to find she has left and he is bankrupt.

The series narrates his attempts to find employment. Though he wants and needs work, no one wants a man of his age; furthermore, he realizes that his academic talents are not needed either. His growing disillusionment is revealed, his gathering despair and feelings of hopelessness. One episode ends with the proud man broken, humiliated and in tears. Yet, from that terrible experience, hope is born – the late starter rises to new life.

The programme summed up for me all the human frustrations, hopelessness and despair. I imagine most of us have entered that deep valley, and maybe some of us are in it now. The cross declares: 'I've been there. I know.' 'My God, my God, why hast thou forsaken me?' That cry was a real cry of despair from the cross – not make-believe.

What about us? I have a hunch that true life starts at the point of recognizing our failure. That is the point when new life begins. 'Unless a grain of wheat falls into the earth and dies . . .' (John 12.24) The importance of death is that for God it is the commencement of resurrection.

The cross takes us into death and failure, but the Greeks had another beautiful idea which is called 'deification'. Irenaeus puts it so splendidly: 'He became human that we might become divine.' He entered into our world to redeem it and restore it.

Jesus our pioneer restores all things and will bring them to a glorious fulfilment. The third aspect shows a connection between this life and the one to come. True Christianity never treats this world with contempt. Beware of any form of faith which says: 'Well, you know this life is unimportant; the real one is the one with God.' No! This life is sacred and is a gift. Of course, the life with God will be glorious, but it will be a fulfilment of all the hopes and dreams here. That is why Irenaeus hit the Gnostics so hard, because they rejected this

life as unimportant. You and I will want to affirm this world
and its beauty and its sadness and all the colours of life – the
greens and golds, the greys and the blacks – as part of the
tapestry which is God's gift to us all.

What about today? How can we weave this theory into our
theology and practice? Let me take you to one twentieth-century Christian who seems to me to express this so vividly.

The man I have in mind is Oscar Romero, who was assas-
sinated the year Robert Runcie was enthroned as Archbishop
– 1980. Romero was the unlikeliest of heroes and this is an
encouragement to us. As a priest and bishop he was not
marked by revolutionary fervour – on the contrary, he was
deeply conservative and disapproved of 'political' priests.
Hold that description of him in your mind for a moment. Now
turn to the country. El Salvador is a poor country of just five
million people; a place where the gulf between rich and poor
could not be greater. Because the clergy were on the whole
ministering to the poor, many of them could not avoid being
caught up in the unrest, violence and fear. Some identified
with a form of theology called 'liberation theology'. Romero
disapproved of this theology; he did not believe that the way
of Christ called anybody to overthrow governments. As he
saw it, the job of the Church was to get on with the task of
proclaiming the gospel and ministering the sacraments.

When he was appointed Archbishop, the Government
sighed with relief. Here was an Archbishop after their own
hearts. Yet soon after his enthronement, Romero's close friend
Fr Grande and two parishioners were callously shot in cold
blood by security forces. Fr Grande's crime? He had preached
a sermon in which he had said these words: 'It is dangerous
to be a Christian in our nation. In fact it is practically illegal
to be an authentic Christian, because the world which surrounds us is founded radically on an established disorder
before which the mere proclamation of the gospel is subvers-
ive.'

The death of his friend became Romero's conversion. He
was outraged and demanded an explanation. He closed all
Catholic schools and colleges for three days and cancelled all
services for the following Sunday, except for a single Mass in
the Cathedral Church, to which 100,000 people came. Events

swiftly followed. Romero was caught up in denouncing
policies which engulfed the poor in further misery and exploitation. He saw that it was necessary to take sides. There was
escalating violence against the Church. Romero became a
symbol of hope to people. When asked: 'Why have you decided to take such a stand?' he replied simply: 'I felt it necessary to put feet on the gospel.'

The climax came when, on 24 March 1980, as he celebrated
Mass, a shot rang out. His blood mingled with the red wine of
the Mass. But it was a death in line with the pioneering Lord
he followed; a fitting martyr's death for a very courageous
man who found that God could be trusted with his weakness
and fear.

III. Jesus – Who Identifies with Us

We are now faced with the question: From what did Jesus save
us?

Let me now go to a number of scriptural passages to see how
the New Testament sees the death of Jesus. Common to all
these verses is the idea that Jesus' death in some way removed
our sin. He became sin for us. This idea developed in the
Church and became linked with a theology which is known as
'penal substitution', the idea that Christ paid the penalty for
you and me. In the divine tribunal he became a sin offering.

In the post-Reformation world the doctrine of penal substitution gathered around it a very hard edge, especially north
of the border in the eighteenth and nineteenth centuries. Let
us now go in our imaginations to Dunbartonshire and visit the
town of Rhu in 1829 where the young minister of just twenty-
nine was preaching. He had been at this cure for a mere four
years but his reputation was growing fast. He was known for
his brilliance, for his razor-sharp mind and for being a wonderful preacher. His elders were becoming more than a little
worried because people were saying his teaching was hereti-
cal. For a start he was preaching that assurance was essential
for salvation; that is, you could know within you that you
were well and truly saved. He was not saying merely that you
believed it, but that you could know it as certainty! Furthermore he was preaching against Calvinism. He rejected John

Calvin's idea that Jesus paid a penalty to God. So on this summer's evening, to an expectant and full congregation, we hear him saying something like this:

> Now I hear some of you saying this: 'Jesus saved me from my sins by taking my burdens himself; he came to this earth to save me and to redeem me.' Oh, yes, we can all agree with that. But how did he redeem you? 'Oh,' you reply, 'he took the penalty for me.' But what do you mean – he took the penalty for you? 'I mean that I should have died that afternoon, but the matchless Son of God took my place. God visited all his wrath, judgement and curses upon Jesus and therefore I can go scot-free.'

> But I want to put another point of view. How can it be that Jesus could become sin for you and me? How is it possible for someone to take my or anybody's sin upon himself? You simply cannot switch *moral* qualities. Of course he came to rescue us, of course he came to die for us, but he was not a sin offering to God because he was sinless. So you ask me: 'How are we redeemed therefore?' I will tell you: He identified with our distress, our despair and our lostness. He became so identified with us that he was the *perfect penitent* and made the *perfect confession* to the Father for us.

The sermon that evening was the last straw. The minister, Dr McLeod Campbell, was accused of heresy and two years later deposed from his office. His theology, nonetheless, was to have a major influence upon atonement thinking, and helped to shape modern thought.

Now, before we look at Campbell's teaching more closely, let me mention another thinker who probably had some influence on him.

Socinus was a radical Reformation thinker who saw Rome as the great harlot of Revelation 17. He was a forerunner of Unitarianism. He viewed Jesus as one who revealed God, but who was only a human being and no more than that. For our purposes we must note one thing: he rejected any connection between our sinfulness and Jesus' death. Moral qualities, he argued, cannot be transferred. God can no more transfer his sinlessness to us than we can transfer our rights or wrongs to one another. So how did Socinus see God's forgiveness operating? Simply in terms of God's free gift. Salvation is not won by Christ but given by God. In Socinus's theology, therefore, there was no room for Christ except as a voice proclaiming salvation. In technical terms we say that Socinus rejected the 'forensic' idea of salvation.

So did Campbell, although he came close to it with his emphasis upon Christ as the perfect penitent who makes the perfect confession.

What does this mean for us? Campbell is arguing that Christ shows God's love by identifying with us in our guilt and sinfulness and by standing before God as a perfect penitent. Campbell is not saying that Christ takes our sin upon himself but he identifies so closely with us that *it is as if* he makes our confession and is thus separated from the presence of God for us. Let us look at this more closely. Is Dr Campbell saying that Christ did not really take our sin upon himself but acted as if he did? That is the crux of the problem. How can Christ be a perfect penitent if he is *really* sinless? Putting it in ordinary terms: if you are completely innocent of a crime, no one is going to make much sense of it if you say: 'I am not guilty of this offence, but I confess on behalf of others and wish to represent their guilt.'

Now, I happen to think that Campbell's idea is flawed because he wants to have his cake and eat it. He wishes to reject the idea that Christ took upon himself our guilt but he wishes to say that Christ identified with our sin and weaknesses. There is, nonetheless, a positive side to his teaching.

Let us think about the word 'identification'. The more you belong, the closer you identify. Think of children. When we moved from Durham to Bristol our youngest daughter was ten. By then she had acquired a distinctive Geordie accent and she was upset when her friends at school teased her about her rounded vowels and up and down, sing-song voice. She felt excluded. How did she react? By acquiring a Bristol accent! Think of teenagers. It has been said of them that 'in order to be different they dress exactly alike'! In fact, you cannot find more conformity than among young people. They are anxious to belong, and it shows in their tastes, dress and habits. But it is true of us all – it is hard to break from the herd, it is hard to be a rebel, it is hard to be a heretic. Identification is part of our survival kit; it is the way we are. To belong is to identify. Think of missionaries who attempt to reach another group of people. In order to have any remote chance of effective work they must learn the language, understand the culture and customs and identify in all kinds of ways with the people they wish to influence.

At the 1988 Lambeth Conference the Bishop of Hyderabad told an apt and amusing story about this. When the troops pulled out of North Pakistan at the end of the last century, the Church Missionary Society sent a missionary doctor to the region to speak to the people of God's love. The fierce Pathans saw this missionary in his little wooden home about a mile away and they said: 'The British sent troops to kill us and they failed. They now send a doctor to poison us.' So they did not go anywhere near the doctor. Months passed and the doctor despaired of ever reaching them. Although he dressed as they did and walked among them, sullen glances were all he got. He even learnt their language. Still no breakthrough came.

One day, the missionary was awakened by the sound of scratching at the door, and the noise of whining. He opened it and there was a village dog with a broken limb. The doctor treated his first patient. Washed and bandaged, the dog limped into the village. 'Who did that?' It could only be the doctor – and the breakthrough came. Then, said the Bishop to the assembled Conference, 'Who was the missionary – the dog or the doctor?' In fact they both were. The doctor with his presence and the dog as the witness to what the doctor had done.

Turning to Campbell's contribution, two ways are mentioned by which Christ identified with us.

First, *Christ identified with our loneliness*. Campbell had no doubt that sin was essentially a form of loneliness; being cut off from God and his presence. The consequence of sin is that it cuts us off from others. It issues in forms of alienation or separation. Christ, said Campbell, accepted a cutting off from his Father in order to unite us to God. Let us think about this idea for a moment.

We live in a society riddled with loneliness: loneliness in offices, in our comfortable homes, on our estates and in our flats. It is a loneliness caused by having no one to talk with.

Perhaps one or two of you have had keen personal experience of the frightening and destructive power of loneliness. Now, by loneliness I am not talking about the absence of friends and occasional breaks from people. In my busy life there are times when I dream of long periods away from people. Oh, to be quiet; oh, to be on a desert island with no one to talk to! But the reality is far, far different, and few of us can take that much reality. I am not talking about that kind of quietness; rather the loneliness of people who feel quite cut off from God, from others, from society. They feel estranged; they feel as if they don't belong; they cannot identify.

Two years ago on BBC television there was a moving programme called 'The Boy David Trilogy'. It was the story of a Peruvian boy from the jungle with almost no face . The programme described David's condition and the sixty operations he had in order to have anything like a face – and there were still plenty to come. But the love that surrounds that boy is having a marvellous effect in giving him a life. His face is still deformed, but it is a face. When Desmond Wilcox teased him and said: 'You're a pickle!' he replied: 'I'm not a pickle, I'm a person.' I was reminded of C.S. Lewis's great book *Till We Have Faces*, which makes the point that each human being is on the way to his or her full development in Christ.

Loneliness is being cut off from God, ourselves, our destiny, our hopes and dreams. Christ identifies with us, and in the garden of Gethsemane he cries out of loneliness for us.

Campbell also speaks of a form of loneliness which was a special feature of Jesus' ministry: *the loneliness of the leader*. All of us in leadership know something of that. 'The buck stops here.' The leader may delegate a great deal of work but cannot delegate the responsibility for that work. The leader carries that alone and carries too the anxieties, ambitions and the fear of failure that leadership brings.

Perhaps some of you are experiencing the pressures of leadership. There are times, of course, when all goes well and we actually enjoy it, but at other times the cost seems too heavy and we have few people we can share the job with or who can understand. So the anxiety mounts and the stress develops. We wake in the night with a churning mind and it seems that nothing will settle the anxiety. Campbell links our problems of leadership with that of Jesus' loneliness, and comments: 'See, he has been there too and because he identifies with it, he can handle it. Don't pretend.'

The second very useful contribution from Campbell is that he saw how *Christ identified with our suffering*. I have used the word 'mystery' of the cross, but let us never forget that suffering is a mystery too. We must never have a simplistic view of suffering. We have all had experiences of life in which the suffering of others has led us to ask questions of God and about God. 'Why are you doing this to me? Where are you in the midst of pain?' Suffering and the cross nonetheless come together in Jesus' prayer of suffering love: 'Why hast thou forsaken me?' (Matthew 27.46)

Indeed, the Christian faith takes very seriously the presence of suffering and says that the life and death of Jesus encourage us to endure. Hebrews 12.3: 'Consider him who endured from sinners such hostility against himself, so that you may not grow weary or fainthearted.' The story of Joni Eareckson is well known. In 1967, as a result of a diving accident, Joni was made a quadriplegic. Bitterness, anger and rebellion became her reaction. One night, Cindy, her friend, spoke to her of the cross of Jesus and said: 'He was paralysed too.' It had never occurred to Joni that on the cross Jesus was unable to move, virtually paralysed. She found that deeply comforting and was mentally able to see that he was carrying her pain and helplessness.

Christianity also takes seriously the fact of *redemptive* suffering. Now we have to be careful with the word 'redemptive' because in a final way only Christ's sufferings can be deemed truly redemptive; but I feel that we can make guarded use of the term. Jesus' sufferings draw us into the love of God and show us how much he loved us. Campbell points out that Jesus' sufferings, far from being heroic, are far more wonderful than that; all our wounds and pains are taken up in his and are redeemed.

Some of you may have read Mary Craig's book *Blessings*. In it she recounts trying to come to terms with the fact that two of her four sons had been born with severe abnormalities. In the last chapter she meditates on the meaning of suffering. She writes:

In the teeth of the evidence I do not believe that any suffering is ultimately absurd or pointless . . . the value of suffering does not lie in the pain of it but in what the sufferer makes of it. It is in suffering that we discover the things that matter; in sorrow we discover ourselves.

So identification is a rich word.

Let me try to illustrate this from the career of one notable Christian. His name was Father Damien of Belgium. In 1864 he unexpectedly took his brother's place as a missionary priest and was sent to Hawaii. His Superintendent asked for a priest to go to the island of Molokai where a colony of lepers lived in appalling conditions. Joseph Damien, without hesitation, volunteered, and for the rest of his life lived among the lepers. The colony increased to over a thousand people. Joseph laboured as builder, nurse, superintendent as well as priest. But the moment of deepest ministry came when ugly spots appeared on his hands and face. One day at Mass Father Damien addressed the community and said simply: 'We lepers.' Damien, no doubt, would not have considered this particularly heroic – all he was doing was following his Master in identifying totally with those he had come to save.

IV. Jesus – Our Reconciler

In this talk I want us to consider an image which I believe takes us a little closer to the meaning of the cross – the image of reconciliation and representation. Let us glance at a familiar passage of Scripture: 2 Corinthians 5.16-21. You will note that the verb 'reconcile' occurs five times – that in some mysterious way God reconciled the world to himself and that Christ was the means and the focus of reconciliation. In what way was he for us the focus?

Some years ago now, a famous Methodist scholar, Vincent Taylor, wrote a trilogy on the atonement. In it he expressed the view that Jesus was our *representative* who reconciled us to God. Vincent Taylor was particularly concerned to avoid crude ideas that Jesus was a sin offering, one who somehow bore the penalty of our wrongdoing and placated an angry deity. He correctly drew attention to the fact that the action was God's – God was in Christ; that is to say, he was doing it.

Let us first look at the word 'representative'. It is a familiar and attractive idea. Recently there has been a long ambulance drivers' strike. Leaving aside the rights and wrongs of that dispute, we all know the importance of representatives. Five thousand ambulance drivers cannot do their own negotiating – they need representatives to do it for them. Indeed, in this country we have a conciliation service, known by its initials as ACAS, which is a forum whereby representatives can get together and make demands, counter demands and eventually – and hopefully – reach solutions.

Let me point out some of the weaknesses in the idea that Jesus is our representative.

First, we did not choose him. We normally elect our representatives and say: 'He belongs to us. He can speak up for us.' In the case of Jesus it might be thought that he represents the management, not the workers. Second, can he really represent me and you unless, in some real way, he participates in our sin and weakness? So we need to ask: Does Vincent Taylor's idea go far enough? I am not rejecting the idea of Jesus being my representative – all I am doing at the moment is to point out some difficulties with it when it is considered as the central idea in the atonement theory.

Now let us consider the concept of reconciliation and note the elements that stand out.

Reconciliation needs someone to take the initiative. The atonement may seem an irrelevant idea these days, but here is an image which is always topical, because the need for reconciliation is a lifelong occupation. One thing I can be certain of is that we have all been involved in rows, misunderstandings and quarrels. Perhaps something like that happened today and you wonder how reconciliation can take place. Often the problems are only storms in teacups, and all that is needed is a gentle 'sorry', a laugh, a hug, a cup of tea, and all is well. Sometimes, however, bitter feuds may last for years. In the course of my pastoral visiting, before I took a funeral service, I called on the dead man's son, who told me that he fell out with his father at his wedding twenty years previously and that he was not going to the funeral service now!

We feel the shock and sadness of unreconciled behaviour that can follow people like that to the grave. It is a fact that

the more serious the crime, and the more awful the act, the
more costly the nature of reconciliation. Let me offer another
illustration. At the end of the last war, the Allied Forces did
not say to Germany: 'War is over, let's forget it all. We all made
mistakes. Build your country and let's live in peace again.' No,
you cannot do things like that. Awful crimes had been committed by a civilized nation because Nazism had put to death
over nine million people. Evil men had ruled with terror and
evil. The Nuremburg trials were the trial of evil and resulted
in judgement. It had to happen before there could be true
reconciliation of nations and before countries could begin to
live and forget.

Now, what the New Testament says is striking. God is never
spoken of as if he needs to be reconciled to us. God does the
reconciling. He says: 'The door is always open. I love you so
much that Christ is the means of reconciliation.' This is where
we must challenge the idea that forgiveness is a costless thing;
that all God needed to do was forgive. He will forgive, people
say cheerfully. That is his business. Some theologians have
suggested that the essence of the gospel is nothing more than
forgiveness as it is enshrined in the story of the Prodigal Son.
The father sees the son coming home after all the bingeing –
the wine, women and song – and runs out with love and says:
'How good it is to have you home! Kill the fatted calf!' That is
the gospel, they say. It is, however, only one half of the gospel.

Forgiveness is a killing business; it has a habit of crucifying
people. We must not minimize the cost of reconciliation; forgiveness is never cheap. But let us ask again: Is it the case that
moral qualities cannot be transferred? If a son or daughter
commits a crime and is sentenced to imprisonment, the court
will not allow an anxious father or mother to take their place,
so how can it be that my sin can be taken by another? How is
it possible for Christ's death to affect me? Let me give you a
partial answer for the moment.

First, we cannot allow human factors to limit God's goodness. God's wonderful grace and power can be made available
for us. Therefore his goodness and grace *are* transferable.

Second, it is a deficient view of sin which speaks lightly of
it. We are of a generation which is in dreadful danger of being
anaesthetized morally. People who are blind cannot judge the
colour of light, people who are totally deaf cannot assess the

wonder of a Mendelssohn sonata, and people whose whole experience of life has been lived in the darkness of materialism cannot fully appreciate the holiness and perfection of God who dwells in light unapproachable. We have lost our sense of holiness and we shift in the shadows; little wonder we fail to understand the significance of atonement! So the cross proceeds from a forgiving God who wants people to be reconciled to him. He does the reconciling, he sees the sin, the hurts, the enormous chasm of unreconciled conflict, and he takes it all to a lonely cross.

Doesn't that say something amazing about God's love? He who is the blameless party takes the initiative in running towards us to forgive.

Reconciliation involves repentance. We have to say 'sorry'. Imagine a married couple who are estranged from one another, yet who both wistfully long for reconciliation. Let us imagine that they meet and the man begins: 'Darling, it's awful to be apart from you. I miss you so much. Can we make a fresh start?' She agrees – she too wants the past to be healed. But the husband continues: '. . . but let us get one thing clear – I haven't done anything wrong!' No human relationship can recommence with such an attitude; there has to be the admission of failure.

So it is with the cross. In a sense we now live in a forgiven world. When Christ died, 'atonement' was made between God and man. At-one. That is still the reality of the Christian message, but that forgiveness only becomes a reality, efficacious, when I make it mine.

The implications of this are awesome, because the Christian life is a continuation of atonement. That is why the Lord's Prayer demands that the Christian community becomes a forgiving, reconciling community. 'Forgive us our sins, for we ourselves forgive . . .' (Luke 11.4) Think of the implications of that! If we are reconciled to God, it affects others. It means that we accept others. Surely we need to work this out in our daily living. Next time you catch yourself thinking uncharitably of another, criticizing another, say to yourself: 'Reconciliation – what does that have to say to my relationship with that person?'

I would like to apply that to other relationships. Think of the fact that there are over three hundred member churches in

the World Council of Churches! Think of all the division in the
Christian family which mocks the idea of us as a reconciled
body. How dare we say with St Paul, 'be reconciled to God' (2
Corinthians 5.20), when we are so unreconciled? Isn't that a
terrible contradiction of the message of the cross? We Anglicans have made our fair contribution of hurts to the unreconciled body of Christ. You see, the cross preaches a radical
message to us all – it proclaims that the ground is level at the
foot of the cross. What about our Church with all the opportunities and challenges before us? Our Archbishop has just
announced his retirement, and whoever is chosen to succeed
him will lead us into the Decade of Evangelism. Among other
things, he will also have to handle with great sensitivity the
issue of women's ministry. Have we the capacity to remain
together even though there may be real theological differences
among us? I hope that the reconciliation achieved by the cross
will provide the basis for us all to say that we have no grounds
for making fresh divisions which make a witness to a needy
world more difficult than it is already.

Reconciliation implies a contract. When two parties meet at
ACAS and an agreement is reached it is normally expressed
in terms of some contractual agreement which satisfies both
sides. In the Bible such an agreement is called a 'covenant'. We
notice this about the covenants of the Bible; they are usually
established with the signs of sacrifice and blood. Abraham's
willingness to offer his only son Isaac has the innocent Isaac
saying in Genesis 22.7: 'But where is the lamb?' Abraham
replies, 'God will provide himself the lamb for a burnt offering, my son' (Genesis 22.8). The Egyptian deliverance has the
sprinkling of blood on the lintels of the doors so that the
avenging angel can see the blood and 'pass over' it (Exodus
12.13). At Sinai blood is sprinkled on the altar and the people.
Barbaric, we might exclaim, how awful! Maybe, but the point
the Bible is making is that 'without the shedding of blood
there is no forgiveness of sins' (Hebrews 9.22). God's way of
reconciliation is harshest for himself in his Son. The new covenant is commemorated every time we celebrate the Eucharist;
and we have a vivid image of the covenant every time we hold
out empty hands to receive the sacrament, because we have
nothing to offer. Indeed, there is no point in offering anything
because we are 'ransomed, healed, restored, forgiven'.

Vincent Taylor draws attention to two striking contrasts in God's method of reconciling. First, he considers the contrast between power and weakness. In the covenant established between God and humankind, God is all-powerful and we are weak. The powerful have a way of establishing contracts that suit them. We have often heard our Prime Minister say: 'We must negotiate from a position of strength.' That has plausibility in the world of political bargaining. God could so easily say that, too, but he does not; he negotiates from a basis of weakness which becomes for us the power of God unto salvation. In the cross God allows his weakness to be our strength. I have already drawn attention to the power there is in weakness and it is often the case that God is able to take ordinary weak things of this world and make them powerful for him.

The other striking contrast is between holiness and sinfulness. Jesus, our holy representative, takes our sin upon himself and identifies with it. You can now see why Christianity is so radical and so down to earth. You can also see why we cannot play at being Christians – because God became human for us and took our humanity up to the throne of God. This does not suggest, I must warn you, that we must dwell on our sinfulness and the holiness of God. While we must take sin lightly we must not live as if we are unforgiven and unreconciled. It is also a fact that very few people actually come into the Christian faith with a deep burden of sin. It is as we travel into the faith of Christ that we grow in our appreciation of his love and of our own deep unworthiness. Anything we do must be prefaced with: 'We are unprofitable servants.'

Reconciliation cost Christ everything and sometimes it will cost us no less. Let me in conclusion just remark on one of this century's Christian heroes: Dietrich Bonhoeffer.

One of the great theologians of this century, Dietrich was a loyal German who had a deep affection for his country. In his travels before the war he came into contact with a French student, Jean Lassère, a pacifist, who encouraged Bonhoeffer to take the Sermon on the Mount seriously, and to live it out fully. Bonhoeffer returned to Germany, but found himself in conflict with the mood of the times when identified with Hitler's arrogance and brutality. He identified with the Barmen Declaration that: 'Jesus Christ is the one Word of God which we are required to hear . . . we repudiate the false teachings that the Church must recognize other teachings and other personalities alongside this one Word of God.'

This was fighting talk. The confessing Church became the persecuted Church. Bonhoeffer, increasingly uneasy with all he was observing, eventually talked with his brother-in-law, who was on the staff of Military Intelligence. His horror was profound when he discovered the extent and depth of the evil perpetrated by Hitler. With great reluctance, Bonhoeffer came to the conclusion that Hitler had to be removed from office and he became party to a plot to assassinate the country's Führer. But the plot was discovered, and Bonhoeffer was imprisoned and hanged on Low Sunday, 1945. In a letter to Bishop George Bell he wrote: 'This is the end, but for me, the beginning of life.'

V. Jesus – Our Substitute

The idea of substitution must be the very oldest of theories that attempts to deal with the question of why Jesus died. It still has its power to fascinate and impress. This theory takes us first to the theme of sacrifice. It is a theme that still means a great deal to modern people even though we have lost the background of a sacrificial system. Consider any gift; I would wager that the gift that means most would not necessarily be the most expensive present but the one bought with sacrifice, expressing care and love. The point about sacrifice is that it represents slog, sweat and tears. So the Old Testament people were commanded to give a proportion of their talents and money to God as love offerings, thank offerings, sin offerings. The gift could vary from pigeons, to cereal offerings, to first fruits of the harvest, to very expensive sacrifices like a goat, a lamb or a bull.

Not all sacrifices were sin offerings. For example, the lamb in the Passover celebration was not a sin offering; it was a communion offering. It represented God's deliverance and was closer to our Eucharist than to a sacrifice. If we are really looking for an archetypal sin offering, we must turn in our Bibles to Leviticus 16, where Aaron presents two male goats before the Tent of the Presence. One is said to be for the Lord and the other for Azazel. Upon the head of the latter goat the sins of the people are placed.

Who was this Azazel? Who knows? Perhaps a figure for evil or the place of sinfulness and evil. As my deliberate intention in these lectures is to remind you of theology and introduce you to theological terms, however, let me do so now. Here is the first theological word: *vicarious*. Vicarious means a 'stand-in', someone who replaces you. So, in the old days, a vicar was a clergyman who did not receive the tithes and proper dues of a parish. He would merely do the job and get a pittance. Someone else would get the perks of office; whereas a rector received the full tithes. These days we have dealt very satis-factorily with the problem; we have made the rector as poor as the vicar! But you understand now what the term 'vicarious sacrifice' means – it means that someone else, or, in the Old Testament, *something* else – a goat, a bull – took your sin for you. The idea of 'scapegoat' comes from this passage (Leviti-cus 16.20 following).

The idea of sacrifice was part and parcel of the ancient world, and familiar to both Greek and Jew. This is clear from a number of New Testament passages: Mark 10.45; John 3.14,16; 15.13; Romans 3.23-25; 5.8-9; 8.32; 2 Corinthians 5.21; Galatians 3.13; Ephesians 2.15-16; Hebrews 9.26-28. In these verses, and I could have easily quadrupled them, we are presented with the idea of Christ dying for us. Sometimes the word is *for us* and at other times *instead of us*; but whatever the word, the New Testament writers were in no doubt that Jesus was Saviour of the world, and that his death was the crucial victory of God.

There are quite a few hymns which take up this notion of Jesus bearing my sin as a substitute. There is, for example:

> There was no other good enough
> To pay the price of sin;
> He only could unlock the gate
> Of heaven, and let us in.

Or a verse from one of St Bernard of Clairvaux' hymns:

> Jesus, who gave himself for you
> Upon the cross to die,
> Opens to you his sacred heart.
> O to that heart draw nigh.

Look at the words of the hymns, glance at the dates and link them in with the theories we have discussed, and I can promise you that it will all make a little more sense and make it even more evident how our hymn-writers wrestled with the meaning of the cross.

The next question is: If Jesus died for me and paid the 'price of sin', to whom was the penalty paid? I challenge anyone to show me anywhere in the New Testament a verse that says Christ pays a penalty. His death is a sin offering, he gives his life for us, he dies for us, but, as far as I can tell, the New Testament never answers this question: To whom is the sin offering given? I wonder why this is?

It is later Christians who will answer the question absolutely and thoroughly. Some of the Fathers of the Church believed that Jesus paid the penalty to the Father. He placated God. Others of the Fathers were in no doubt that Jesus paid the penalty to the devil. Yet stay with the problem: how could Jesus pay the price to the Father when the Father was involved so directly in the work of the Son? Don't you see now why the substitutionary atonement must not be forced, because it separates the Father from the work of the Son? Taken to an extreme, it makes the Father sadistic and the Son a Saviour who dies to placate an unforgiving Father. That is surely wrong, and we must never adopt any theory which severs the Father's will from the work of the Son. In any case, the words of Scripture contradict such ideas. 'God so loved the world that he gave . . .' (John 3.16), 'God was in Christ reconciling the world . . .' (2 Corinthians 5.19).

So here is mystery with a vengeance – we seem to have the attractive idea that Christ died for you and me, he went to the utmost limit for us, he gave everything away, and in some mysterious and tantalizing fashion he took my sin and yours upon himself, but we cannot say to whom the price was paid! Have we any clues? Let me offer some.

The first clue we have lies in the concept of participation. The theologian R.C. Moberly's *Atonement and Personality* helps us, I believe, with the analogy of a human family. Think of a child who is alienated from you. I am sensitive to the fact that some of you will understand the problem more powerfully than any illustration, but I will press on. We might imagine a young person very defiantly rejecting the family, taking drugs and living with someone. Yet there is not total rejection; the young person feels shame, guilt and bewilderment. The problem, suggests Moberly, is how to create a change of attitude in the child to bring them back again. It would be no good to wave the law at them; it would be no good to whisper 'there, there'. There is only one way, and it is a costly way. You have to bear the punishment by standing with them, taking the shame with them, and bearing the cost with them. This, says Moberly, is what Father and Son do for us: they enter into the pain of human sin and lostness and suffer with us and for us.

The writer D.E. Whitely has in his book *The Theology of the New Testament* a powerful image of an officer in the war who had to lead his troops across a dangerous minefield. He knew he would lose many of his men in the dangerous, slow pathway across. There was one way, however, only one way he could make sure no life was lost apart from his own. Deliberately he walked into the minefield, triggering off every mine and thus absorbing in his own body the entire explosion. Like every illustration, of course, it only goes part of the way in satisfying our minds. I want to go further.

This takes me into atonement as vicarious love. Our problem is that we always separate love from justice and love from holiness. Going back to the family problem just mentioned, much as we love that child in spite of his problems, we would not let ourselves be completely taken over. The idea of our homes being smashed by drugs, by prostitution, by evil of whatever kind, would most surely be unacceptable to us. We would say: 'Much as I love you, I cannot condone this behaviour. This is wrong.' Here we are at the heart of the problem: holy love. Love which wants redemption, healing, forgiveness and reconciliation knows that the demands of justice have to be met. There is an eternal law which reduces in utter simplicity to: 'You shall love the Lord your God with all your heart, and with all your soul, and with all your mind . . . and you shall love your neighbour as yourself' (Matthew 22.37,39).

I heard someone say the other day that modern people treat

the Ten Commandments like examination questions: only
four need be attempted. The Ten Commandments nonetheless
stand as the expression of God's holy Law and of the purity
and goodness he demands. How we fail it, time and again! It
is in holy love that we glimpse the meaning of the cross
because 'God so loved the world that he gave his only Son'
(John 3.16). God's love is outgoing, outpouring love. It is a
love which redeems sinful people, not by saying: 'We'll let
bygones be bygones', but by saying: 'I'll bear that load for you;
you won't need it again.'

It seems impossible, then, to avoid the New Testament
message that Jesus' death was planned by God to be the means
of reconciliation and peace. God, who does not need reconciling, becomes the Reconciler; God, who does not need appeas-
ing, becomes our peace; God, who knows no sin, becomes sin
for us – by whose stripes and wounds we are healed. In the
death and resurrection of Jesus the two gardens of Eden and
eternal life are joined.

What are the implications for us today? Let me mention just
two.

The Church must put the cross back into its preaching. Over the
last fifteen years, preaching has moved, by and large, from
preaching the truths of the Christian faith to the experiences
of the Christian faith. The Holy Spirit and his power has been
a favourite theme, or 'You too can build a splendid church, or
be an excellent minister, if you buy this book or follow these
ten lessons.' A 'cross theology', not on its own, let me add, but
central to our preaching, will take us back to the central verity
of our faith. We are not in the business of popularity; it is too
bad if others do not like the cross. But ignore the cross and you
ignore true Christianity.

Yesterday I and a few of my colleagues spent a day's retreat
at Compton Durrville, a Franciscan retreat centre in this
diocese. You cannot go to a Franciscan centre without coming
face to face with Francis' emphasis on the cross. You who
exercise a ministry of preaching and teaching, do preach the
cross as the starting point of hope and peace. Don't be
ashamed of its offence to the proud hearts and minds of
self-sufficient men and women. They need its message of
hope, pardon and peace. I don't think we will talk sensibly
about a Decade of Evangelism if we give a cross theology

second or third place in our preaching.

We must put the cross back into our spirituality. Bonhoeffer, the theologian to whom I have previously referred, once remarked in one of his books: 'When Christ calls a person, he bids him come and die.' That goes to the centre of our faith. We are dead in Christ. Paul describes it vividly in Romans 6 in the theology of baptism. Enter the waters, and you die with Christ and rise to newness of life. In a wonderful way that is a thrilling thing to take on board. From a Christian perspective, you and I will never face death. Christ faced it for us and was victorious. Our mortal bodies may die but we will never die. We are already enjoying eternal life, and physical death will merely mean the passing from life, in which we see through a glass darkly, to life when we shall see and know as we are known.

If I am already dead and alive in Christ, then I must embrace the cross with a greater vigour and commitment. I must try to live under the cross daily. I must put my Saviour always before me as my example, friend and guide. I must live a life that pleases him. The problem is that it is hard. A friend once remarked: 'We are expected to be living sacrifices, but the problem is we keep crawling off the altar.' How right he was! How necessary it is for each one of us to apply the cross to our daily lives – to our giving to one another and to God of our money, our time, our talents. Skin-deep Christianity will not endure, but heart Christianity will, because it is marked with a cross.

A cross spirituality will ensure that you and I are never tempted to follow fashions and fads in church life which, attractive though they may seem, ignore the cross or push it to one side. Recently I have been reading the writings of Matthew Fox, a Dominican who is very popular for his creation spirituality and love of the environment. I agree with a great deal of his concerns. But I notice this: he exaggerates creation above redemption; sin is treated as a rather tiresome preoccupation of the Church, and what matters is the sin and fallenness of mankind's abuse of creation. This is a distortion of Christianity which never separates creation and salvation in that way. True Christianity believes that creation itself is fallen and awaits its redemption; that it also will benefit from the perfection that Christ offers and achieves.

A cross spirituality is, however, far from miserable and world-rejecting. Christ was never that. Just as he moved with grace, strength and love among men and women, so the Christian under the cross and the Church under the cross will have an effective, attractive and powerful ministry if we show his grace and live in his strength.

In this series I have been introducing twentieth-century martyrs to illustrate the points I have been making. The theme of substitution is graphically revealed in the story of Father Maximilian Kolbe, a Roman Catholic priest who died in Auschwitz. A prisoner had escaped from Auschwitz and ten prisoners were required to die in the starvation bunker – block 13. Names were read out. The tenth person cried: 'Oh, my God, my wife and children.' Suddenly Father Kolbe stepped forward, a small emaciated man with round glasses, and addressed the Commandant. 'Let me take his place.' The other prisoners gasped because they expected him to be shot on the spot. The Commandant, equally surprised, asked: 'Who are you?' 'I am of no consequence, only a Catholic priest, doing my duty. Let me take that man's place, please.' He nodded, and the condemned men were sent away to the starvation bunker.

One man who was attendant to the condemned men said that cell 13 became like a church. Instead of the screams of starving men, there were prayers, and the prayers passed into silence as one by one they died of starvation a few yards away from food. Only Father Kolbe remained alive until a bored guard gave him a fatal injection of carbolic acid.

It would not serve my purpose to make that an illustration of Jesus taking my place or yours, because God the Father is clearly not like a Nazi war criminal. Yet there are two points of contact. First, Kolbe's death brought meaning and hope to dying men. It showed the importance of human dignity and love. Christ's death was that to an immeasurably greater degree. Second, it was an amazing act of faith. It could have been such a futile act. The man whose place he took could have died the following week, or the next month. It seemed such a pointless act of heroism. But it wasn't. The man survived the war and told the tale and has lived a purposeful life ever since, seeking to carry on Kolbe's work of reconciliation. I sometimes wonder if there was that kind of risk when God planned the cross from the beginning of time. I think there was and is. R.S. Thomas has a lovely poem, 'The Coming', which seems to suggest that.

> And God held in his hand
> A small globe. Look, he said.
> The son looked. Far off,
> As through water, he saw
> A scorched land of fierce
> Colour. The light burned
> There; crusted buildings
> Cast their shadows: a bright
> Serpent, a river
> Uncoiled itself, radiant
> With slime.
> On a bare
> Hill a bare tree saddened
> The sky. Many people
> Held out their thin arms
> To it, as though waiting
> For a vanished April
> To return to its crossed
> Boughs. The son watched
> Them. Let me go there, he said.

Conclusion

Kolbe died for his friend and Christ died for us – as an example for us to follow, as a pioneer who goes before us, as one who identifies with us, as our reconciler, as our sacrifice, and as our substitute. As such he demands our response and our commitment. That is why I keep saying that I am not only interested in our knowing more about our faith but also in our putting more faith into our lives. May we all say with St Paul in Galatians 2.20: 'I have been crucified with Christ; it is no longer I who live, but Christ who lives in me; and the life I now live in the flesh I live by faith in the Son of God, who loved me and gave himself for me.'

16

Easter Day: The Challenge of the Resurrection
Wells Cathedral, Easter Day 1988

Karl Heim, German Lutheran theologian, scientist and writer, recounts an incident which occurred in Moscow shortly after the Russian Revolution. One of the frequent mass meetings attended by workers was taking place. The leader announced at the beginning that complete freedom of speech was allowed but speeches must be kept short. Many speeches were delivered expounding the glories of communism. When all had finished the leader asked if any wished to represent the other side, since they had promised freedom of speech. A little under-nourished priest climbed the steps. As he did so the chairman called out 'Five minutes, please!' He replied: 'I won't need five minutes for what I have to say.' Then he began: 'My friends, you have heard all the arguments that have been brought forward to prove the new world-view. But, my friends, Christ is risen!'

You might have expected a howl of derision to greet this cry, but it did not come. The workers had heard those words many times before at the Russian Easter night service. So on this occasion when the priest set forth this ancient cry, it was as if a sleeping volcano erupted. From a thousand voices came back the response: 'He is risen indeed, Alleluia!'

Now was that priest simply playing cleverly on the emotions of the crowd? I don't think so. He was challenging the so-called 'newness' of the Revolution with the 'newness' of the resurrection. He was, of course, touching a nerve deep within the Russian psyche, but he was saying something like this, that 'if Christ is risen, every argument for atheism is flawed'. Now I personally have every sympathy with the man who says sceptically: 'Dead men don't rise!' Of course they don't! But what we find in the resurrection of Jesus is not something that originates from the natural processes of life, but something that constitutes a unique event. It is a breaking in of something wholly new: it is an act of creation which parallels the story of creation in Genesis 1.

Years ago I read a sentence which has remained with me through the years. 'The resurrection of Jesus Christ is the first article of the Christian faith and the demonstration of all the rest.' Now this may not be characteristic of modern Christianity – more the pity for it – but I do believe that it is a just reflection of New Testament Christianity, because in the earliest preaching the emphasis falls on his resurrection. The last act of Jesus was the starting point of the preaching.

For years I found it very odd that the disciples spent very little time talking about the significance of the death of Jesus or even the person of Jesus. The emphasis falls instead upon the resurrection. The reason seems to be that the gospel story was formed backwards. Instead of starting with the birth of Jesus and going on to his ministry, death and resurrection, the first disciples began with the resurrection and showed how it made sense of the rest. The notes of excitement and joy pervade the pages of the Acts of the Apostles. Here we find the ring of truth because if you were one of the disciples and Jesus had appeared to you, what would you have told your friends? You would not have gone to them with a theory of the death of Jesus – you would have gone to them with great wonder saying: 'It is incredible, but our Lord is alive. He lives and all is well!'

This great event is the foundation stone of the Christian Church. It stands or falls on this one event. While, of course, the universal symbol of the Christian Church is a cross and rightly so, the cross is Part One of the Easter story. When Jesus died, faith in his message died as well and his movement, which had begun with such promise, collapsed. If the figure on the cross had been the last sight of him, we would have heard nothing more of him and there would have been no Church. But from this broken and scattered group of men and women came the startling message of the cross and resurrection with a conviction and power that neither the Jewish authorities nor the Roman rulers could stem. Well did one writer say: 'The evidence for the resurrection is the existence of the Church in that spiritual vitality which confronts us in the New Testament.' This is so. If you were to take a pencil and cross out every verse in the New Testament which refers to the resurrection or to the idea that Jesus Christ is alive, you would not have much of the New Testament left. It throbs with the conviction that Jesus was raised by God and is alive for evermore.

What does it mean for us today? Let us consider two ways in which the resurrection of Jesus challenges us today.

First, it challenges our world-view. That priest was right. The cry 'Christ is risen' is a challenge to secularism and materialism. It proclaims that this is God's world and that his values are all that matter. But it is not only the atheism of communism that is challenged by the resurrection, the materialism and secularism of our own culture comes under attack as well. Even we as practising Christians find it extremely difficult to avoid the acid of materialism. The delights of a secular society seem so appealing; technology appears to deliver the goods. Indeed, for many of us, we have never had it so good. That is, until we start to look at the reality of our society. The erosion of values and moral standards, the relativism of life, the shocking things that happen, reveal that our civilization is but a veneer that hides a viciousness and rottenness that frighten us all.

The Easter story calls the Christian Church back to identify uncompromisingly with the death and resurrection of Jesus Christ. Of course we shall get howls of laughter. The death and resurrection of Jesus Christ is an uncomfortable message. It is still foolishness and a stumbling block. Lose the resurrection hope, though, and we lose our way. Even this great cathedral will become a museum and mausoleum the day we lose our confidence in the resurrection.

Second, we are reminded that while the evidence for the resurrection is impressive, first Christians did not merely believe in the resurrection. They did not simply see an empty tomb and say: 'Coo, he must have risen!' They did not go out giving intellectual addresses saying: 'Come to our seminar and we'll discuss the epistemological significance of the empty tomb.' They rushed out with a testimony: 'Christ has appeared to me! He is alive! I know it for myself!' You can't keep good news in. I remember years ago being amused when a young man given to very few words came to our vicarage and burst in with the news: 'Jane had a baby boy this morning!' still with his bedroom slippers on. He could not keep the good news in. It had to be shared.

Some years ago I saw Sister Gemmell of the Church Army on television. She was then working among 'down and outs' and prostitutes in London. She was asked if she believed there was life after death. She replied: 'No.' When the interviewer leaned forward open mouthed, she went on: 'I don't believe, I *know* there is life with Jesus, after death takes my mortal body.' She had experienced the risen Christ and she knew. In a similar way the famous psychiatrist Carl Jung, when asked about his belief, said: 'I don't believe – I know, I know.'

I believe that for some of us there's the need to possess for ourselves that inner conviction and excitement that is a mark of New Testament Christianity. That conviction came very late in life to the Victorian writer and theologian R.W. Dale. It was said of him that he was preparing his Easter sermon early one Easter Day when the significance of the resurrection dawned on him. For years he had preached it, he had believed it intellectually, but never had it become personal to him. This eminent theologian rushed out into the streets to greet the astonished passers-by with the words: 'Christ is risen, he is risen indeed!' It makes all the difference. If Christ has not risen from the grave of our lives, from our doubts, fears, from our personal deaths, then all the so-called evidences of the resurrection are of no consequence except as props. Jesus Christ's resurrection has to become *our* resurrection if it is to mean anything at all.

This morning I would like to invite everyone to face up to the challenge of the resurrection. It calls us to identify with a Christ who through the horror of the crucifixion leads us, his people, to new life and hope. It will make a difference to our world-view, to the way we see people, to the way we view God. With the countless multitude of saints down the centuries we will be able to unite in exclaiming: 'He is risen indeed – Alleluia!'

17

Ascension Day: All will be Well
Wells Cathedral, Sunday after Ascension, 27 May 1990

The readings about Jesus ascending to his Father raise very serious questions for the Christian. Do we really believe that he ascended? If so, does that make him the first cosmonaut?

You can understand why there have been attempts to question the doctrine of ascension, because it seems to assume that heaven is a place above our heads and that Jesus somehow rose up there to an unknown physical location. I want to suggest that we should put such notions from our minds. The most probable explanation is that we have here an acted parable, in which Jesus returns to his Father in the only way that the disciples would have recognized as departing, and that was by going from them physically. Of greater importance than the *manner* of his going is the *meaning* of his going. Let me tease out four meanings of central importance.

Ascension means that *the work of the Son is finished*. The epistle to the Hebrews mentions that when Christ returned to his Father, he sat down at his right hand. The words 'to sit' mean that his work was completed. This rather ignored festival of the Ascension in actuality brings the Easter story to a close. Christ's work of restoring humankind to God was finished and the message of the cross and resurrection is made vividly clear by the ascension. We are 'ransomed, healed, restored, forgiven'. Our Great High Priest has completed his work of salvation and he now represents us before our Heavenly Father. The message we bring to others is therefore a very hopeful one: we are able to say to people, *not*, 'if you do your best you may after enormous struggle find the mercies of God; if you go to church all your life you will graduate to the presence of God', *but*, 'You and I are already accepted by him as dear children and the only movement necessary is to reach out and receive what he wishes to give us.'

Ascension also means that *Christ is present*. Have you noticed that however wonderful a trip may be, going home almost seems the most wonderful part of it? As the plane lands in one's own country, as the car takes you up familiar lanes or roads to that well-known door, you look at your companion and say: 'It's good to be home.' But in the returning home you are not the same; you have been enlarged and enriched by the experiences you have shared and the new friendships made. For the people abroad you have met, they too have rich memories and are now enlarged through those moments of meeting.

In a much more significant way the coming and returning of Christ meant that. Before the ascension Christ's presence was limited, local and confined. He was present in one place only. After the ascension Christ is present for everybody. You can see now how our language fails to describe the richness of this event. I said a moment ago that he departed, but in fact the ascension declares that he is with us always. This introduces a thrilling idea. We often think that our job is to bring Christ to the world. We hear evangelists talking about bringing Christ to others. Well, we know what they mean. But Christians do not have to make Christ present, he is already here. Our job is not to bring him to others if he is already here in our world, in our institutions, in our brokenness and sin; our job is to make him known, to reveal him in all his splendour. He is with us now and he does not leave us after we leave the House of God but journeys with us through life, leaving his touch whenever and wherever we share his presence with others.

There is a third meaning to ascension that I would like to explore with you: *our humanity is accepted by God*. I love the words of the epistle: 'In saying, "He ascended," what does it mean but that he had also descended into the lower parts of the earth?' (Ephesians 4.9). The language and imagery may sound foreign today, but the meaning is clear – there is no part of human life which is untouched by the presence of God and by the possibility of his redemption. The darkest areas of human experience and life are known to him and are within his reach. Yes, our fears and doubts; yes, this world in all its frailty; yes, Terry Waite and others in that Lebanese jail; yes, our worries about ourselves, our families and our children. All these and more are his concerns and we must never fall into the trap of thinking that anything is unredeemable.

Finally, ascension means for me that *all will be well*. I remember one of my clergy telling me that in his parish he had had a number of deaths, one after another, and this had really got through to him. We all know about that; you feel somehow diminished yourself. Then came another blow, the terminal illness of one of his closest parishioners and friends. He remarked: 'You know what it is like, Bishop, you begin to wonder where God is in all this.' He went to St Margaret's Hospice, feeling very miserable, to see this lady who was dying of cancer. His gloom must have communicated itself to her, because she looked up at him and beamed and said: 'Don't look so miserable, Vicar, I'm only dying!' He told me that those words put it all in a Christian perspective. All is well if Christ is risen.

If you get the chance to go to that marvellous play in London, *Shadowlands*, do go and see it. The story of C.S. Lewis and his late romance with Joy Davidson, a lively American, is a poignant and moving story of her fight against cancer and the changes this makes to Lewis himself. The play describes how Lewis, and even his theology, is changed by this vibrant lady. C.S. Lewis firmly held to the view that this life, and even the deepest of our relationships, are but shadows compared to the reality and riches that lie ahead. As Joy lies dying, she whispers to him with typical humour: 'You'd better be right!' He was, because that is the message of ascension. The reason why in our Gospel reading the disciples were in the Temple praising God was because they knew what we easily forget, that Christ's ascension did not mean his departure from us; it meant his arrival home and the assurance of his presence in every part of creation – and with us today.

18

Pentecost: The Birthday of the Church

Bristol Cathedral, Pentecost 1983

Just the other day in College I was discussing the significance of Whit Sunday with a group of students. I said: 'Today, the Holy Spirit does not come – usually, that is – with a great noise from the skies, with tongues of fire touching everyone and the whole company being filled with the Holy Spirit and speaking in other tongues. So', I asked, 'how do we discern the presence of the Spirit today? Give me a profile of his action.' A lively discussion ensued, and the following three points were agreed.

First, we recognize the Spirit's presence by the quality of *life* in the congregation. I well remember the birth of my youngest child, Elisabeth, eleven years ago. There she was in my wife's arms, a passive little thing – but what held my attention were her eyes. She looked at me as if she were thinking: 'Hello, who are you?' I don't know much about what a baby takes in at that stage – precious little, I suspect – but her eyes indicated that she was a living intelligent being, and so she has turned out to be. The Church, as I said, is the child of the Spirit and it will, if it is under the Spirit, show forth the Spirit's life. At a very basic level that quality is manifested in the way we live as Christians. Paul says in Galatians 5.22-23: 'The fruit of the Spirit is love, joy, peace, patience, kindness, goodness, faithfulness, gentleness, self-control.' Of course, Paul's analogy is taken from the idea of life in the tree and the sap rising to feed the branches and fruit.

Jesus made a very similar point in his conversation with Nicodemus who came to have a private chat with him about religion. Jesus looked directly at him and said: 'Unless one is born anew, he cannot see the kingdom of God' (John 3.3). 'How can a man be born when he is old?' exclaimed an astonished Nicodemus. 'Truly, truly, I say to you,' said Jesus, 'unless one is born of water and the Spirit, he cannot enter the kingdom of God' (John 3.5). Now I am sure that, with me, you have experienced the embarrassment of those words 'born again'. We have all been accosted by zealous Christians who have perhaps thrust a leaflet into our hands and asked: 'Are you born again?', or 'Are you saved?' Their approach may well be objectionable, their understanding may be blinkered and naive, but they are reminding us of the Spirit's work in our faith and life. He is at the heart of what it is to be a Christian. Long before the Holy Spirit became an article of the creed, he was a living reality in the experience of the primitive Church.

Second, with my group of students, we agreed that the Holy Spirit was *unpredictable*. Perhaps at first we have to live with uncertainty, and only after a period of turmoil and waiting do we begin to recognize his working, sometimes in unexpected areas of the world or Church. One doggerel I love goes like this:

> There was an old man who said, 'Run,
> The end of the world has begun!
> The old Holy Ghost
> Is the one I fear most,
> I can handle the Father and Son.'

How true this is! We all, especially theologians, like to pigeon-hole God's activities. We want to codify God and his way with us and wrap a nice bow around it, saying: 'God works like this, God can be found in this way. If you do such and such, you can find God's peace, his power.' As we know so well, it doesn't work like that. By any human standard, the Holy Spirit is untidy and unpredictable. He just will not conform.

What does this mean, then, for us? I think it means that we must ask for discernment to recognize his ways in the world. I suppose this is another way of saying that the Church desperately needs to recover the ancient gift of prophecy. We have many preachers, speakers, committees and so on, but we don't have enough men and women with prophetic insight who can point us to where God is at work and what he wants us to do. Our modern dilemma is well summed up in John Taylor's fine book about the Holy Spirit called *The Go-Between God*. He writes:

> But while we piously repeat the traditional assertion that without the Holy Spirit we can get nowhere in the Christian mission, we seem to press on notwithstanding with our man-made programme. I have not heard recently of committee business adjourned because those present were still awaiting the arrival of the Spirit of God. I have known projects abandoned for lack of funds, but not for lack of the gifts of the Spirit.

How right that is, and how we need to question whether it is God's will to do the very good thing we have before us as agenda item no.4.

What we do know is that the Holy Spirit's work usually commences unpretentiously and quietly. Who would have guessed the outcome of a young man's protests against the worldliness of the Church in the early Middle Ages? His name was Francis and his home was Assisi. No one in his right mind then could have predicted that his movement would have become a worldwide organization which would make a lasting impression upon Church and society. We could go on picking examples from history. The problem is that it doesn't help us today. We have to keep looking and, like the Church before the day of Pentecost, waiting in prayer.

Third, my group of students wanted to identify the Spirit's ministry with *unity*. His symbol is the dove, the expression of peace, and yet the disunity of the Churches mocks our common agreement that the Spirit is at the heart of unity. More seriously, our disunity contradicts the message of reconciliation we claim to bring. How can we go to a divided world with the news that Jesus Christ saves and gives peace, and that he unites all things through the blood of his cross, while we show so blatantly that we Christians cannot get on together? A Muslim saying is that where you find ten Christian denominations you find eleven different sets of opinions! We are shamed by such valid comments and our mission is silenced by disunity which contradicts the reconciling power of the gospel. We compound the folly by closing circles around our-

selves. Roman Catholics question Anglican orders, we question nonconformist orders, they might question one another
and we cannot meet together around the symbol of unity
which is the focus of our redemption.

I am sure personally that if the Spirit is doing anything in
the Church, his most pressing problem is the unity of his
people. Yes, I believe that great things are happening, but not
a lot will change unless we change in our attitudes to others
and unless the Spirit gives to us accepting hearts and ears that
listen to the insights of other traditions. The story in Acts 2 is
meant to convey the truth that when the Spirit comes he unites
all in him and in Christ. The crowd gathers, the church proclaims with power, and they all come together to hear the
wonderful deeds of God. Well did a theologian from the Greek
Orthodox church say:

> Without the Holy Spirit, God is far away,
> Christ stays in the past,
> The Gospel is a dead letter,
> The Church is simply an organization,
> Authority a matter of domination,
> Mission a matter of propaganda,
> The Liturgy no more than an evocation,
> Christian living, a slave morality.
>
> But in the Holy Spirit
> The Cosmos is resurrected and groans with the birth
>   pangs of the Kingdom,
> The risen Christ is there,
> The Gospel is the power of life,
> The Church shows forth the life of the Trinity,
> Authority is a liberating service,
> Mission is a Pentecost,
> The Liturgy is both memorial and anticipating,
> Human action is deified.

And that is what we celebrate every Pentecost.

19

The Challenge of Ministry
*Three talks given at a Training Conference for the Clergy of
Bath and Wells, 1989*

I want to share with you a mixture of theology and practice on the theme of 'The challenge of ministry'. I must confess to an abhorrence of theology divorced from real ministry, and an equal dislike of ministry separated from its roots in theology, because such a divorce has no basis in the Bible or the great Fathers of our Church. If that is not ambitious enough, then what follows is sure to be, because my intention is to bring together three insights from three great traditions in our Church – Catholic, Evangelical and charismatic – and I shall attempt to relate them to the fourth Gospel in which these insights are to be found.

Our three themes are 'Incarnation', 'Proclamation' and 'Spiritual Renewal'.

I. Incarnation

I need not tell you that John's Gospel is one of the most sublime and yet most complex books in the New Testament. However, it presents very awkward questions to the New Testament student and faces the fundamentalist with intractable problems especially to do with historicity and facticity. Its way of looking at Jesus Christ seems to clash with the Synoptics, yet very few scholars and students would ever consider casting this book aside, because its testimony and its teaching reaches us in a way that few other books do. Long ago Clement of Alexandria called it the 'Spiritual Gospel' and so it is.

Starting from the opening statement, in which testimony is

given to the Word who became 'flesh', the theme of incarnation is a dominant theme in this marvellous Gospel. Central to it is the word 'glory' (*doxa*); but here we have a surprise. For us glory is so often associated with dignity, prestige, riches, the applause of men, the pomp and circumstance of the world. In John 'glory' is linked with concepts to do more with shame than splendour.

Three things stand out. First, there is the association with weakness. In spite of John's high Christology, Jesus in John 4.6 is tired and thirsty; he weeps at the death of a close friend in John 11.35; he is in need of succour at his death in John 19.28.

Second, there is the link between weakness and his death: 'Unless a grain of wheat falls into the earth and dies, it remains alone; but if it dies, it bears much fruit' (John 12.24).

Third, glory is linked with faithfulness to his Father and obedience to his Father's will. 'I glorified thee on earth', chapter 17 begins, stating the completion of an earthly ministry which had been expressed in manifesting God's name to others and identifying both with his Father and with those he came to serve.

So in John 'glory' is not that of the glory of a divine being who glides through the world, like a character in 'Dallas', but one whose glory is only properly understood in terms of humanity, weakness and identification.

I need not tell you that in Christian theology and history the doctrine of 'incarnation' has been a very important element of Catholic theology and spirituality. Whereas Evangelicalism has had a tendency – which can sometimes be a weakness – to over-concentrate on the death of Jesus and his finished work, the Catholic tradition has majored on the theme of incarnation and has seen this as a crucial paradigm for ministry.

What, therefore, are the elements of an incarnational theology that bear upon the challenge of ministry today?

Earthing the Gospel

One of John's emphases, as we saw earlier, is on the humanity of Christ. He 'dwelt among us' John 1.14, and in that context, John writes, 'we have beheld his glory.' The incarnation strikes the note that God did not dictate terms from afar but came into human history and suffered and died in the person of his Son.

It has long been a mark of Catholic life and thought to make incarnation a central element in ministry. For example, Leo XIII's Encyclical of 1891, *Rerum Novarum* ('On the Condition of Working Man'), was a Magna Charta of Christian social ethical theory. We could also point to other significant documents such as Pope John Paul II's social statements in *Redemptor Hominis* and *Laborem Exercens* for equally splendid examples of incarnational theology.

In practical terms, however, what does 'incarnational ministry' mean? It means risking everything for God; it means accepting the place where he has put us as the place of incarnation for us; it means recognizing that the most important thing you can give others is yourself. Of course, people want your gifts, your learning, your culture and your talents. All that is self-evident; what is not always said is that they want *you*, and that is the most precious gift you and I can offer. Anyone who came from the East End of London as I did will need no reminding of the work of the outstanding Anglo-Catholic priests of the East End in parishes like Poplar, Whitechapel, the Isle of Dogs, and so on. Although I knew none of them personally, my parents used to tell me tales of the sacrifice, love, and humour of such men who gave themselves to the poor people of the area.

Incarnation was, of course, central to the thought and life of the great missionary Bishop Frank of Zanzibar. When a young man came to him and wanted to join the Mission but excused himself by saying: 'I don't think I should live in Africa', Frank responded swiftly: 'I didn't ask you to live – you can glorify God by your death!' You cannot get an earthier gospel than that!

Weakness and failure

When I was Principal of a well-known theological college I was struck one day by the fact that most of my students came from successful churches like St Aldate's, Oxford, All Souls', Langham Place, Emmanuel, Northwood, or one of the many flourishing Evangelical churches. This began to disturb me, not because I was opposed to such spiritual origins – indeed one wishes such vocational direction was true of other churches – but because I wondered if such young men and women had any idea of the reality of authentic ministry today. In a

great number of cases their only experience of ministry was
the booming, lively worship of such places followed by the
equally supportive, intimate and womb-like experience of the
theological college. 'How could we', I mused, 'prepare them
for opposite experiences – when prayer is not answered; when
opposition comes; when the numbers in the congregation are
small and discouraging; when personal weakness is experienced in all its startling intensity – sexual, psychological,
physical and spiritual? How will they cope with the greatest
opposition of all – apathy?'

I believe that the incarnational model of ministry helps us
to see that weakness and failure, rather than being extraneous
aspects of ministry, belong in fact to the soil in which true
ministry is rooted. Take weakness. The incarnation stresses
that it is our very weakness that has potential for the Kingdom
of God. When you or I accept our personal weakness as integral to our ministry, we are truly accepting something which
anchors us in New Testament ministry, as we see from Paul's
experience in 2 Corinthians 1.

Let us look at failure. Surely that is not a mark of ministry?
Are we not called to be successes? Well, so we may have been
taught. Look again, though, at the incarnation of the Lord.
There may be found the signs of disappointment as only one
of ten lepers came running back to thank him; when he was
rejected by his family and home town; when at the end of his
ministry he wept over the city of Jerusalem and cried: 'Oh
Jerusalem, Jerusalem, killing the prophets and stoning those
who are sent to you!' (Matthew 23.37) We fail our congregations and certainly our ordinands, if we give them the impression that authentic Christian ministry usually results in
success, strength and life. While I for one would not want to
doubt for a minute the fact of the new creation, this is not to
suggest that it implies a 'Superman' view of the Christian life
– that from now on life is renewed and sin is a thing of the
past. An acceptance of weakness and failure is a pre-condition
of Christian growth and maturity. I learned years ago that if
the Christian faith means anything at all, it means that God
accepts my weakness and failure, and this very unlikely context becomes the vehicle of his grace and strength.

Presence

Incarnation means 'God with us' and, as I mentioned earlier, in John's Gospel there is a strong emphasis on Jesus manifesting God's name and manifesting the 'real presence' of God among his people. It is therefore hardly surprising that integral to the elements like food, drink and human companionship, love and mercy are irradiated with a new glory as they are taken and given to God. Let me explore very briefly with you three ways in which God manifests his presence among his people, even today.

First, there is the 'real presence' of Christ as we minister to others in his name. I was not surprised, although I was disappointed, to get the results of a recent survey of clergy time in a neighbouring diocese which revealed that 60 per cent of all clergy time is taken up in administration. This is a shocking percentage of our time – and the same survey claimed that only 15 per cent of clergy time was spent in visiting. It is fashionable to deprecate visiting because, we are told, it is a waste of time. No one is at home when you call and, anyway, it ought to be the job of lay people! Well, it may be very true that we must encourage lay people to play their part in visiting, but don't be fooled by such talk. How can we preach with any degree of effectiveness if we don't know our congregation, if we are not there at important moments of their lives, if we are not seen around in the community and don't take part in secular pursuits? Tom Allen, the Scottish evangelist, said in the 1950s about effective ministry: 'You must earn your right to speak.' That right can never be earned by time spent only in church, office or home.

Second, the body of Christ in the local community has great potential to be a 'real presence' as it ministers in different ways. The over-spill of Sunday worship in Monday to Saturday commitment is the nature of congregations relating gospel to community. No worthwhile evangelism ever takes place in a vacuum, and few disciples will be made by a church alienated from the community in which it is set. Making connections with the social, political and cultural life around is simply being faithful to the gospel.

Third, in an important way our church buildings are 'sacramental expressions' in which God manifests his love and glory. I am a passionate believer in the importance of keeping

churches open for prayer and worship. I have long been convinced that hearts can be stirred and wills can be changed by
church buildings lovingly cared for in which prayer has
become 'valid' through generations of faithful and loyal worship. Let us not despise the physical or become iconoclastic in
seeing the spiritual as expressed only in non-physical ways.

Why then do we need an incarnational ministry? I am not
saying that this is the way of growth – no, it may not be that,
although I personally believe that a church which takes this
seriously has very real chances of growing numerically. I am
saying that this appears to have been the pattern of Christ's
ministry and should therefore be at the heart of ours. I invite
you to recall with me that the way of ministry is the way of
the cross, and the way of the cross is that of glory – glory
wrapped in humanity, weakness and presence.

II. Proclamation

Now we move into the area of 'Proclamation'. This is, as we
know, a familiar theme in the fourth Gospel. The Christ of this
Gospel is the proclaimed Christ – indeed the whole point of
the Gospel is to point to him as Saviour and Lord. Consider
the haunting words of John 3.16: 'For God so loved the world
that he gave his only Son . . .' Consider the evocative words of
the Greeks saying to Philip in John 12.21: 'Sir, we wish to see
Jesus.' It goes on: 'I am the way, and the truth, and the life'
(John 14.6) until the climax of the story: 'These things are
written that you may believe that Jesus is the Christ, the Son
of God, and that believing you may have life in his name'
(John 20.31). John's Gospel, therefore, is a vast confessional
document, from faith to faith, written so that the person of
Christ may be known and followed. In John, Jesus comes
across as a preacher, calling men and women to know him and
to be drawn into his life.
    Now it is common to associate preaching and proclamation
with the Evangelical tradition and, to be sure, it is authentically and keenly there. The Evangelical tradition is, quintes-
sentially, the tradition which exists to promote the 'evangel'
(good news). While it is true that it runs the risk of falling into

fundamentalism on the one hand and anti-Church on the other, its genius lies in its Christo-centricity. I want to suggest, however, that such an emphasis is not and cannot be the possession of one tradition alone. It belongs naturally to genuine priesthood and ministry. Just as an incarnational approach to ministry must be shared with the whole Church, so Evangelical zeal and Evangelical proclamation and preaching must be possessed by us all. Gregory the Great once said: 'Whoever comes to the priesthood undertakes the office of a preacher.'

And we all desire to be better proclaimers of faith because we can see so clearly around us the spiritual poverty of people, their lostness and despair. We wonder sometimes how preaching can in our modern world regain its power and authority. I certainly do not come with instant answers as to how such a thing may be, but I suggest to you that to be effective proclaimers of Christ, we must hold in tension four major elements which I consider to be key elements in the task of ministry.

Being and doing
None of us, as I have mentioned already, can become an effective preacher unless we are anchored securely in a life of prayer and worship. The greatest men and women of God were made strong through a daily walk with God. I often find that my greatest insights come from ordinary things like the beauty of nature or human activity. Take the time last year when I was working in a neglected part of the garden and I came across a bedraggled *Spirea* bush, choked by an evil bindweed. I had to clear the weeds away, feed it with the right food, cut it back and give it time and space to grow. A year later it is a different bush, healthy and strong.

So it is with my spiritual life. I need space to think, to take in, to brood on good reading and to meditate and pray. The regularity of a daily office and private prayer will be, as it were, the clearing of the weeds and the cleansed and renewed space for my activity. From this quiet centre, reflection on the task of preaching will become its reservoir and strength; ideas will come from this source, and God will be given the chance to make our preaching a 'sacrament' through which his grace may be expressed. But it will only be an effective sacrament if we relate the 'being' side of our ministries to the 'doing' side.

The natural and spiritual

The story is told of a Victorian academic who, after preaching a totally abstract and boring sermon, popped back into the pulpit and said: 'I'm awfully sorry, but for every reference to Aristotle, please substitute St Paul!' That approach contrasts sharply with that of our Lord whose preaching was earthed in real life. His sermons began where people were – the natural impinged on the spiritual; heavenly ideas were expressed in earthly idioms and concepts. He illustrated from life and drew upon daily experience to clothe his teaching. Think of the vivid, concrete images that Christ used in his teaching – flowers of the field, camels going through the eye of a needle, a woman who has lost a valuable coin, the abandoned father, the lost sheep – all these and more show a master communicator in action, skilfully drawing on the experience of others to make his point.

This should be the pattern for us, and we must struggle to find ways of connecting with people and their needs. Speaking personally, from my earliest days as an ordinand, I have been an unashamed collector of stories and illustrations from whatever source is at hand. All around us is the reservoir of good things – in nature, in films, in books, in daily newspapers, in television soaps, in the theatre, and so on. Be on the look-out for ways of enlivening your talks and addresses. Charles Spurgeon used to say that if people fell asleep in his talks, that was not their fault but his, and he had to do something about it. I once heard an undergraduate remark: 'I don't know if professors talk in their own sleep, but they certainly do in other peoples'!'

The application for us is obvious. If I am called to be an ambassador, then I am forced to ask: Have I made it clear what I am driving at? Have I spent sufficient time in honing my skills as a communicator for the glory of God? Have I attempted to communicate by using concrete illustrations?

Interest and intelligence

You may know this line in one of Dryden's poems:

> The midwife laid her hand upon his skull
> with this prophetic blessing: 'Be thou dull.'

If the Christian message is as exciting and life transforming as we Christians claim it is, then how dare we make it dull and lifeless! So it is up to you and me to make sure that our proclamation is interesting, lively and sometimes provocative. In so doing we must never underestimate people's knowledge or intelligence. Don't protect your congregation from hard thinking or difficult questions. Within certain limits, let them see you sometimes exploring the frontiers of your faith and facing up to difficulties. A preacher who never credits his hearers with struggles, doubts, fears and failings will never properly relate to their real needs or be able to meet them.

In order to relate interest and intelligence successfully, we must be constantly fed and our minds alert. We know how hard it is to keep our reading up to date. Indeed, in the parish ministry with all its demands it is a constant struggle to do any reading at all. But we must, if we are going to feed others and equip them for their ministries in the world. Our tools will obviously include the Bible and exegetical aids. Scripture must be and become our major textbook. Its witness must guide ours and its concerns for the building of God's Kingdom must shape ours; but with this obvious cornerstone, read widely. Don't be a dilettante, dipping into slight books of experiential faith. Keep your mind alert by having a heavy book on the go, and draw upon the rich resources of theology to grow as a thinking person yourself. This will keep you alert and help intelligence and interest to engage for the benefit of your listeners. Such study will avoid the danger expressed in the doggerel about the 'one-sermon' priest:

> Ten thousand thousand were his texts,
> but all his sermons one.

Simplicity and profundity
The constant challenge of preaching is how to bring together two seemingly opposite ideas, simplicity and profundity. In other words, how can I speak clearly of the things that lie ultimately beyond my comprehension?

Apparently it was Goethe, the writer and poet, who remarked to a curate who had preached a sermon loaded with
doubts and questions: 'Young man, it is certainties I need, I
have doubts enough of my own.' Whatever the background to
that story, no preacher has the right simply to share doubt or
share faith – your job and mine is to share what we know of
the good news and to lead others to the person we worship
and serve. Here simplicity and profundity must combine. I
must tell the story with a directness and simplicity that befits
a gospel which is good news for all. So much preaching is too
vague and convoluted. One student at a theological college
submitted a sermon to his Principal with the question: 'Will it
do, sir?' 'Will it do what, my boy?' came back the disconcerting answer. We are called to preach Christ and we must do it
well, confidently and directly.

Simplicity, however, is never the same as simplism. Simplicity is refreshing clarity which highlights what you want to
say, leaving your hearer in no doubt whatsoever of your
meaning. Simplism is almost its direct opposite: under the
guise of simplicity, it obscures the depth of a truth by its
attempt to get back to basics. Our Lord was a simple preacher
although no one could have accused him of simplism. Indeed,
parables and pictures were ways in which the mystery of faith
was expressed.

Let me give an example from my parish ministry. Some
years ago a lady came to see me in great distress. She told me
that she had a deformed child and that she had gone to see her
parish priest seeking comfort. Being an intelligent person, she
wanted some theological explanations. The minister, after
listening intently to her story, greeted her with the brutal and
appalling response: 'Well, what wrong have you and your
husband done to deserve this?' Such naive responses alienate
people from the Christian message because they cannot rightly conceive that God should act in such a way. I am not
pleading for intellectual sermons, but I am strongly pleading
for intelligent, thoughtful sermons which relate to experience
and draw upon the richness of Christian theology.

So does that mean that we can never preach with conviction
or expect God to act? No, far from it; but we must take seriously a world in which there are shadows and shades of grey,
and not always blacks and whites; a world sin-shot and yet

one in which God is working through his grace; a world in which we play our part.

This combination of simplicity and profundity perhaps suggests that our preaching should develop the parabolic approach of Christ, who often stopped short of providing full answers, and whose preaching was often suggestive, inviting the listener to react, argue and question.

So, where the 'incarnation' model invites us to be, the 'proclamatory' model invites us to be a herald and prophet, calling the Church and world to conversion and change.

Let me draw out three implications for us as I close.

First, *we are called to be holy*. Holiness is more than a state of purity; it is a way of life, a commitment to an ideal and personal integrity that takes in intellectual as well as moral formation. This drives home the question: How can I preach the demands of the gospel unless I am under that message myself? A herald must obey his call. There has to be consistency between what we preach and what we are.

Second, *we are called to be teachers*. If I am to aim for excellence as a teacher, then I must sit at the feet of Christ the teacher, and all the saints, and grow in knowledge of Scripture and truth derived from it. I must be alert to ideas and concepts from the world around that might help the listener understand. Then, most importantly, I must have the humility of the learner and, through the pain of criticism, learn how I may become a better communicator of the truth I follow.

Third, *we must hone the tools of our trade*. I must seek ways of becoming a 'workman who has no need to be ashamed, rightly handling the word of truth' (2 Timothy 2.15).

III. Spiritual Renewal

The writer of the fourth Gospel has been described as 'the greatest New Testament interpreter of the Holy Spirit'. I would unhesitatingly agree with that statement. The Gospel is rich in allusions to as well as descriptions of the Spirit. He is the indwelling Spirit (John 7.39); the Spirit of the new creation (John 3.8); the Spirit of Jesus (John 15.26); the Spirit of guidance (John 16.13); the Spirit of ministry (John 20.21).

Before we make connections between the work of the Spirit and ministry today, let me offer some general reflections on the Holy Spirit.

First, the Spirit is the *God who goes before*. He is not only the 'Go-Between' God, to quote Bishop John Taylor's revolutionary book, but he is the one who is ahead of us. Now this makes a doctrine of the Spirit very difficult indeed. It is a mistake when some sections of the charismatic tradition posit such a detailed description of the Person and work of the Holy Spirit that you would think they were discussing a very predictable and, sometimes we might think, a rather tired middle-class Western gentleman! No, the third person of the Trinity is ultimately mysterious; he is at work in creation and the Church, ceaselessly recreating and going before us all.

Second, he is the *Great Disturber*. John, talking of the new creation, uses terminology reminiscent of the creation of the world when Jesus speaks of the Spirit as 'wind': 'the wind blows where it wills . . .' (John 3.8) So to live with the Spirit is to be driven; perhaps it is to live dangerously, on the knife edge of experience and faith. Perhaps it is to live with the provisional and to be content with living with uncertainty. This is very difficult for many of us to accept because we ache for security in our lives, our churches and our faith.

Third, he is the *Great Christ-Glorifier*. In the fourth Gospel we note that the Spirit's attention is on Christ (John 16.14). Again, while undoubtedly we must thank God for the charismatic movement in drawing attention to the Person and work of the Spirit, let us remain suspicious of any branch of it which moves the centre of attention away from Christ and all he stands for. To do so is to shift the emphasis where the Holy Spirit would not wish it. A truly 'charismatic' theology is one where Christ is uplifted and promoted.

So with these preliminaries, let us explore three areas that bring together the work of the Spirit and the challenge of ministry today.

Spiritual renewal and vision

At the heart of the charismatic movement is an emphasis upon renewal. Of course, there have been many renewal movements in the Christian Church and we should not be dismissive of new movements that promise life and change. The central difference with the charismatic movement is that renewal is associated with the activity of the Spirit, and with its accompanying claim that people need to be Spirit-filled in order to possess all the blessings that God has in store for his people.

Such a vision as this involves the need for *spiritual leadership*. We are told today, again and again, that the Church of England is in crisis, that we are in terminal decline and disaster is around the corner. We need to take this very seriously because the facts of the great retreat by all denominations stare us in the face. We have only to go into our inner-city areas to see evidence of this: derelict churches on street corners witness to the faith of now long-dead people; churches have been given over to warehouses and even to the worship of other gods by people of other faiths.

I can think, in addition, of five major pressures on our Church today. First, congregations are scattered and small. In a diocese such as ours we are only too well aware of this which can so easily lead to the 'Elijah complex' – 'I only am left to worship Yahweh and bear the burden of ministry'. Second, there is the pressure of indifferent communities all around us who take the Church for granted. Many people today still continue to believe that the parish church is their church and would be horrified if they felt cut off from it – but commitment to it is marked in terms of occasional attendance. Third, we have the presence and rise of non-Christian faiths. No longer can we act or think as though the only religion that matters in our culture is Christian – we have to take on board the fact of pluralism in all its shapes and forms. Fourth, we have seen over the last ten years the rise of the house church movement with its confident Evangelical and charismatic message. We may be suspicious of its fundamentalism and sometimes its anti-ecumenical stance, but no one can deny the vigour of its life. Fifth, we have the fact that maintenance of historic buildings often imposes a crippling burden on small churches leading to weariness, dispiritedness and a shift of drive from mission to maintenance.

Nevertheless, in spite of these problems and challenges, to speak of the demise of the Church is very premature. Matthew Arnold remarked pessimistically in 1832 that 'the Church of

England no man could save'. That refrain has been taken up by many people since, although in many ways it is arguably the case that our Church is in better shape than it was in his time – in spite of the five pressures facing us today! Yes, our Church is changing rapidly and the crucial question remains: Have we the vision to see beyond what now is and to work for a more vibrant and spiritual Church?

This is where clear spiritual leadership comes in. Two particular qualities are needed today. First, we have to come to terms with the reality of a situation which has changed our ministerial context from that of pastoral ministry to that of mission. The former Archbishop of York, Dr Blanch, once told a group of Ministerial Selectors that the criterion for selection could no longer be that of finding pastors for a settled parochial ministry. In a memorable phrase he said: 'We are looking for men who can lead the mission of the people of God.' I would want to modify that to 'men and women', but the point is well made. We need leaders who can work and pray for growth; who can lead mission – a mission that belongs properly to the entire body of Christ. Such leaders will have the confidence and faith to believe that congregations can grow numerically; that lives can be changed through the power of God; that God's Kingdom can become a reality even in the darkness of a secular world.

A second quality is that we have to come to terms with the fact of change and all that that means. President John Kennedy once remarked: 'The only certain and immutable fact is that nothing is certain or immutable.' This is the harsh reality of life. The realistic Christian will live with the fact that ministry takes place in a changing world, and effective service comes to terms with this. Of course, we resist it strongly because the forces of conservatism in all of us strive for peace and quiet. In Trollope's book *Clergymen of the Church of England* the Archbishop says wryly: 'We hate an evil and we hate a change. Hating the evil most, we make the change – but we make it as small as possible.' So we do. Therefore to cling to the past, however precious those traditions have been to us personally, may be to cling to the wreckage of things broken by the tide of change.

This is not to reject the past, of course. The Church never lurches from new thing to new thing but reacts to change gently. Managing change is one of the greatest skills a leader can acquire, and for the Christian leader it is to help people to come to terms with changes in liturgy, in the use of church buildings, in the dynamics of human communities and human groupings, in social changes and their implications for church membership, and so on. In all this we look to the Person of the Holy Spirit to guide his Church and assist us in interpreting the signs of the times.

Spiritual renewal and surrender to God's will

In John's Gospel, John the Baptist brings his ministry into relation with that of Christ in the moving words in John 3.30: 'He must increase, but I must decrease.' In my more sceptical moments I sometimes wonder who we are really serving. Who is my ministry for? Whose glory are we really seeking? These are deeply troubling questions because they touch a nerve in all of us. I am glad that charismatic renewal has challenged the Church on this issue, calling us to a deeper commitment and a greater love. I want to suggest to you that this involves me and you in a threefold surrender.

First, we need to make sure that the real centre of our ministries is Christ. This goes back to my question: Who are we really serving? We know only too well that none of our motives is truly pure. In all of us there is a hunger to be affirmed, to be recognized, and for our gifts to be noted. I see nothing essentially wrong with that. If you and I pour out ourselves in service to others, we need others to encourage us and to reassure us that it is not all in vain! Recognize that instinct within you and be grateful for the applause you will sometimes get – and rightly too. Then having got it, inwardly deflect it as the moon deflects the brilliance of the sun, and give the praise to God. 'He must increase, but I must decrease . . .'

Second, we need to give God our ambition. I need not tell you that there are a lot of very ambitious people in the Christian ministry, and the scope for misplaced ambition is immense. A great deal of this is understandable. Let me take you as a representative group. Many of you came into the ministry from promising careers in other professions, and the hunger to succeed can be a very powerful force in each of us. It may come in a variety of forms: the desire to have a wealthy parish, to have the name of being a success, to be unpopular, to be known as a holy person, to have your name in the papers, even to desire higher office in the Church. I have on my desk a very simple couplet which I read some years ago and which is a constant reminder to me to give to God my ambition:

> Perish every fond ambition, all I've sought and loved
>   and known,
> Yet how rich is my condition – God and Christ are
>   yet my own.

I have already mentioned that wonderful man of God, Bishop Frank of Zanzibar. In a biography of him there is this moving epitaph: 'He could accept the day of small things because he had a vision of what things were to be.'

Third, renewal and surrender extends to my family and loved ones. Here I want to share with you some questions that I still encounter in my personal discipleship. They stem from the fact that anyone who attempts to walk the pathway of the cross soon learns that others dear to us are caught up in the sacrifice. Take the time when I was on the staff of a theological college and enjoying my work immensely. I worked long hours. One day my wife asked me to collect my eldest child from school. Walking back with this eight-year-old girl she suddenly asked: 'Dad, do you love me as much as you love your work?' Just as pain cannot be described, I cannot tell you how I felt then that my dearly loved daughter should feel second best.

I have brooded a great deal since on the relationship between discipleship and family life. The call of Christ beckons me to recognize that Christ's claims must always come first, but they inevitably catch up our loved ones in the embrace of that calling. Most of the time that is not a problem until our very enthusiasm for the work leads us into a selfishness that makes unwarrantable demands upon others closest to us. Discipleship must never be an excuse for neglecting our families. That innocent remark by my daughter led to a transformation of my priorities so that I gave time and space to my wife and children.

If you are married you too will have to give attention to this question: How do I bring together that call to follow with the

needs and demands of family life? I want to suggest that we
must have a sacramental approach to our time with our loved
ones as much as we have to our professional ministries. Don't
feel guilty about taking an occasional evening off, in addition
to your day off, in order to spend time with your wife and
family, or your husband and family. You must endeavour to
share your fears, your failings and your hopes with the person
closest to you so that you are not dividing the family by
overwork or neglecting your ministry by over-indulgence.
Our ministries can be so absurdly demanding that they can
take us away from our families, and this can have the tragic
effect of taking them away from God.

Let me now make the same point to those of you who are
single, because the pressures are the same but the problem is
different. It is so easy to pile yourself into your ministry so
that you have no time for ordinary things. Please do not
neglect the fulfilment of your humanity and the space you
need to read, to go to the theatre, to seek companionship and
to share with others. For the single person, the root problem
is that of loneliness, and this can be a double trial in a ministry
which by its very nature takes people away from a 'nine to
five' existence. For all of us, married or single, the practice of
ministry will never be easy – even though we can be sure of
the power of God in it.

Spiritual renewal and priesthood
Let me remind you of our Anglican theology of ministry and
priesthood. All ministry flows from Christ and his body and
exists to serve him and it. That is to say, our priesthood is
derivative and does not belong to us as an inalienable right.
So when we celebrate the Eucharist in the sanctuary, or preach
from the pulpit, or pastor his people, or lead the mission of
the people of God, we are doing it for him, for others and with
others. This has two particular repercussions on our ministries.

First, if my ministry flows from him in his body, then that
precious gift of ordination to the ordained ministry, though
permanent, has to be maintained, jealously guarded and daily
renewed in holiness and spiritual refreshment. I owe it to
others to say with John the Baptist: 'He must increase, but I
must decrease.'

Second, I must recall that God has chosen a weak, fallible person to be the servant of others. As such, I stand with those I serve, and I must resist their call to climb on to a lonely pedestal; I must identify with their concerns and share their humanity. I must remind them of their dignity as members of the 'royal priesthood'.

Conclusion

We have thought about three aspects of the Christian tradition – Catholic, Evangelical and charismatic. I resist all attempts to divide such wonderful contributions to the body of Christ and I find in myself the desire to embrace each of them. That of *incarnation* calls me to identify with the One whose glory lay in suffering and death. That of *proclamation* calls me to be a herald calling others to faith and repentance. That of *renewal* invites me to be open to the power of God, to the dynamics of change and to the future.

20

The Ministry Today

Three Bible readings given at a conference of the
clergy of Bath and Wells, Swanwick, June 1989

I. Ministers of the Kingdom

In these Bible readings, I want us to consider the nature of
Christian ministry from a biblical perspective and its implications. In this first Bible study, we shall look at Luke 4.16-30
and consider the ministry of Jesus. We will ask the question:
What *was* and *is* at the heart of his concern?

The passage in Luke 4 is well known, but I find that whenever I go to it I find new things that I had never seen before.
This familiar story of Jesus' sermon in Nazareth is, in fact, the
earliest account of any service in a Jewish synagogue. Luke
narrates the graphic tale of Jesus the preacher returning home
from ministry in Galilee – the place of the Gentiles – and going
to the synagogue; a place familiar to him from his childhood.
Perhaps Jesus was down on the reading list for the day, who
knows. What we do know is that after the prayers, after the
recital of the Shema, there came the reading from the Law and
then a reading from the prophets. Perhaps Jesus signalled that
he wished to read it, and so the book was handed to him and
he read, most probably the set passage from Isaiah 61. Then
the unusual happened. He closed the book, returned it to the
attendant, sat down – the mark of a teacher – and said: 'Today
this Scripture has been fulfilled in your hearing' (Luke 4.21).
But, as we know well, the story concludes in uproar because
the message was too sacrilegious for words. Why was that?
What was going on? Why was Jesus rejected and deemed
unacceptable?

First, we observe *the character of the King*. Why was Jesus rejected? The answer is to be found in his character. What I find fascinating in the earliest portraits of the Lord in the Gospels is the studied emphasis on Jesus' identification with us. Now it is impossible for us to know the inner workings of Christ's mind. We don't know what anxieties and insecurities he possessed before his ministry began. But I have always tried to maintain as high as possible a doctrine of his humanity and I think there must have been questions in his mind as he was led into a deeper and deeper understanding of his vocation as Saviour and Lord.

So on the one hand we find statements in the Bible which express the nature and purpose of the Lord. For example, that statement in Matthew 1.21: 'You shall call his name Jesus, for he will save his people from their sins.' Then Luke 2.49 tells us that as a boy of twelve he was with the teachers of the Law asking questions and reaching the conclusion that he must be in his 'Father's house'. Yet on the other hand, at his baptism, which was for him also his ordination, he might have had other unspoken questions: What is this all about? What do I do? Where is my Father leading me? His Father responds by telling him who he is: 'Thou art my beloved Son; with thee I am well pleased' (Luke 3.22).

Now, I want to return to this point later, but note for the moment the importance of identity for Jesus and all of us. *Personal identity precedes vocation and gives it shape and substance.* God declares, 'You are mine.' In other words, ministry flows from a sense of personal identity with the Father. So when we look at this passage in Luke 4 we can see the element of identity peeping through very clearly. Verse 18: 'He has anointed me' – perhaps a reference to his baptism. Note also verse 21. After Jesus had handed the book back to the attendant he said: 'Today this Scripture has been fulfilled.' There you have the substance for the rejection that is to come, because the King is revealed; his identity is shown clearly.

It is, nonetheless, an ambiguous identity, isn't it? It was certainly clear for the Lord, but not for the Jews who listened to him. After all, they knew him as the boy Jesus who was the son of Joseph. He played with their youngsters. The horrifying conclusion they might have come to was that, if Jesus was to be believed, God identifies with the poor and needy and reveals himself there! Here we find a strong reference to the nature of God's salvation which is still unpalatable to human beings. We don't mind God trumpeting revelation from the skies; we don't mind God going to great expense to make himself known; but we cannot stand a God who humbles himself to the extent of becoming like us. Yet that is God's way and it is the scandal of Christianity. It is also the scandal of ministry because true ministry is always incarnate in real situations.

So we see two things appearing of the greatest importance to our ministries. True vocation is based on our *identity* and that *identity* is found where God places us. Most of us here have one thing in common. We have many, many differences, but we share this wonderful thing in common: our vocation to serve God as deacons and priests in his Church. Before the questions came, God himself said to us: 'You are my child and I am ordaining you to serve me.' In a very thrilling way we enter into the ministry of the servant, and in Christ's ordination to priesthood we find our own. Some of us have come to this conference very dry, very perplexed, and perhaps disillusioned and dispirited. We admit that we have lost our way a bit and the fatigue of ministry has stripped us of our energy, enthusiasm and love. I hope that we shall recapture the sense of the Lord saying to us: '*You* are my beloved son, with you I am well pleased.' Then perhaps he will grant to us that security of knowing that wherever he puts us in the ministry, our calling is to do it well for him.

Let us look, secondly, at *the character of the Kingdom*.

Consider for a moment the fivefold character of the message of Jesus. Just as politicians talk about their political manifesto, here is the manifesto of Jesus:

Good news to the poor; release to those imprisoned; new ways of seeing; liberty for those oppressed; proclamation that now is the acceptable time.

And he sat down and said,'Today'.

I am afraid that I do not go along with commentators who say that Jesus had only spiritual realities in mind. While they are clearly there – and we must not fall into the trap of thinking that only physical healing matters – I cannot believe that our Lord is not thinking of wholeness in all its shapes and forms. He is saying: 'The Kingdom is here in my ministry. I am the fulfilment of the agelong dream of the prophets.'

Now here I find a disturbing and exciting challenge to our ministries today. We are all talking about a decade of mission and evangelism. But what in reality is the message we are trying to communicate? A tired message that 'if you come to our church you might find some fellowship if you are lucky; that, honestly, we want you to come to our church because we need you more than you need us; that we are not sure what we are trying to sell, but it once meant something special to us and with a bit of luck it could be good news for you'? You know, I think there is a lot of truth in those speculations.

I have just finished reading Golda Meir's biography *One Life*, the exciting story of the rise of Israel. Who could have thought, back in 1921 when she was one of a few thousand people in Palestine, that within fifty years the State of Israel would be a reality? Thanks to people who believed, who never let go of a dream, who lived and died for their faith, that dream became a reality. It is the remarkable story of a people who refused to let go of a vision, but who followed it through great adversity until it became a solid reality.

Am I not right in saying that we follow a greater Lord? Where is our vision for today? Can we say confidently that this manifesto is still true today; that whenever men and women turn to the living God there they find in him healing, forgiveness, wholeness and salvation? If this is not the case, then I fear that a decade of evangelism is nothing more than empty rhetoric, words echoing around buildings vacated by the Spirit.

Yet, can anyone doubt that our society and the societies of the world need a message such as ours! Look at the terrible needs of the human family: spiritual poverty, brokenheartedness, oppression and blindness. Sin makes us poor, sows destruction in our hearts, contaminates human relationships and makes us captive. So here is a real challenge in our hearts. This is our faith – but does it thrill us in the way it used to? Is our love for our Lord still strong? Is the sap of faith still rising in us?

Finally, let us look at *the character of the opposition*. Why did Jesus arouse such antagonism?

There are a number of reasons for it. First, if he had kept himself out of the message he would have been on safe ground. But he did not only preach, he said: 'The spirit of

Yahweh has anointed *me*, has sent *me*.' Jesus came not only to preach a solution but to *be* the solution. That message is still unpalatable to many today. I guess that the deeper and deeper we go into inter-faith dialogue, the more disturbing we shall find such uncompromising statements.

Then secondly he said: *'Today'* – and that must have horrified them. Today; not coming shortly, or next year, but today, now! While his contemporaries were waiting for signs for the messiah, Jesus declared that God's will to save was immediate and that the means was himself.

Thus the admiration of the citizens of Nazareth for this young preacher, who was making such an impact, is changed into criticism and fury as it becomes obvious that Jesus, not content with simply preaching the promised redemption, was taking it upon himself to say: 'Salvation is now available and I am the Saviour.' The fury which tossed him out of the synagogue was the first step along the way that led inevitably to the cross.

It is sometimes a very revealing thing, when studying Scripture, to put yourself in the position of the hearers. In what ways, for example, do we find the message of Christ unpalatable for us? When do we find ourselves wanting to drive him out of our churches for the things he says? Do we sometimes find his words uncompromising and want to dilute them and take away the sense of outrage that they sometimes convey? Perhaps his lifestyle challenges ours; his deep love for the outcast reveals the poverty of ours and the walk to the cross makes us realize that our ministry is not incarnational enough.

Christ's example challenges us in many ways, but if there is just one thing I urge you to hold on to, it is the identification that is at the heart of his ministry. He was called to *be* before he was called to *do* – and because he was called, he was equipped for service.

II. The Ministry of the Church

I want us to look at the Church of Jesus Christ; that wonderful and sacred mystery. Charles Gore once wrote of the Church of England that: 'It is an ingeniously devised instrument for defeating the objects which it is supposed to promote.' Well, we all know that. We have a curious love/hate relationship with the Church militant which, for most of the time, is not militant at all. In Ephesians 4.1-6 we have a beautiful and challenging picture of the people of God and the calling we are meant to possess. It begins 'I, therefore, a prisoner for the Lord, beg you to lead a life worthy of the calling to which you have been called.'

For the sake of convenience I want to take the little word *'worthy'* as our key word. Now we must put this passage in context. 'Therefore' reminds us what has gone before. Paul has spoken of the power of God. Look at Ephesians 3.14-21 to see the power working within us!

The writer, however, brings it all down to earth with a big bump because life is not always up there in the clouds. The harsh reality of church life is the reality of people who do not live grace-filled and grace-full lives, but Christians like you and me who struggle with the reality of being 'graced' people but sinful people. The lower nature drags us down to where we came from. The reality of the Church is certainly that of *simul justus et peccator*.

Verse 1 tells us why it is necessary to live worthy lives, because we are prisoners whose service is perfect freedom. We are slaves of Christ – not free, yet as free as we shall ever want to be. Paul goes on to tell us what it entails: lowliness, meekness, patience, forbearing one another in love. Here is the harsh reality of living the faith. You see, this was at total variance with respectable thought of the day. The civilized world of the first century felt that a man was to be despised who did not believe himself to be the best. You did not humiliate and degrade yourself – after all, there were enough people around to do that. Paul's logic, however, stemmed from the reality of the Christian faith. No one was worthy anyway to stand before God, so humility was the proper place for the slave.

Now we all find this very difficult! Noel Coward once remarked: 'I can take any amount of criticism as long as it is undiluted praise.' But the Christian must be prepared to take the position of the servant; to be abased so that Christ may be lifted high. In one of his books David Watson tells the story of preaching a sermon in a church. He felt it went very well and he was waiting, as we all do, for a word of affirmation. It came. A lady rushed up and said: 'O Mr Watson, the best sermon I have ever heard' – and David said he prayed, 'O Lord, give me humility'. The prayer was answered all too quickly because she continued: '. . . was when so-and-so came last year!'

We have already seen how the word 'transcending' is used to denote the way the gospel helps us to get above the petty ways that our grovelling little egos seek to feed themselves on crumbs of pride and self-seeking adulation.

What Paul is doing is reminding his readers of the reality of the Christian life. If Christ died and was raised by God to life, then life can never be the same again. We have to live resurrection. Gandhi once remarked to a group of missionaries: 'Jesus Christ I admire and revere – but you Christians do not live like him.'

Now look in verses 4-6 at the remarkable emphasis upon oneness. Paul rams home the unity that God desires. I have a theory, based on verses such as this, which is that whatever we may do, we can never break the unity that already exists in God. We look at the terrible fragmentation of the Christian Church, and none of us needs reminding that the 300 member churches of the World Council of Churches is an awful contradiction of the Christian doctrine of reconciliation. Paul, I think, is saying something like this: 'Maintain the unity that you can never really break – there is one God, one faith, one Lord, expressed as it is in the one baptism' (that is why theologically we should never talk of rebaptism). But it is a curious paradox, isn't it? It reminds me of William Temple's saying: 'I believe in one holy, catholic and apostolic church – but regret that it does not exist!' No, it doesn't here on earth, but in the promises and destiny and hope of God it is moving towards its renewal and unity which is a trinitarian unity of love, power and peace.

I want you to notice that there is something that Paul says we have to do: we have to 'maintain' unity. Have we really taken it on board in our parishes that unity is a thing that we must fight for fiercely?

In verse 3, Paul adds something more: we should be 'eager', enthusiastic in keeping the bond of peace. Like a belt, peace is at the heart of the Church's life because Christ is our peace and has broken down the walls of partition. Don't you see, there is no point in fighting; war is over. When you are in a quarrel, feeling resentful and bitter, give in – what does it matter? Christ is risen! He is a worthy Lord: look at the description here in verse 6. 'Above all and through all and in all.' Paul may be saying: 'See how extensive our salvation is; it takes everything in.' I am attracted to another idea: that there may be a reference here to the Trinity. The Father who is above all; the Son who is God through all; and the Spirit who is God in all. Here is the objectivity of the faith which puts all our worries and fears into proportion. The Church may be that body which is but a poor shadow of what God wants it to be, but he is in charge and our job is to live the faith.

Now Paul introduces a different thought. It is all very well talking about worthy living and a worthy God, but how do we live the Christian faith and how does the power of God move from him to us?

We have no time to go into the argument in verses 7-10 which is based on Psalm 68.18, but Paul's thought is that of a victorious army returning home to Zion with the spoils of a battle in their train: slaves and precious possessions; returning heroes with gifts for their loved ones. Paul uses this as a beautiful metaphor of what God is doing for us. Christ descended and he ascended, and through that ascension the power of the Spirit is poured out on all people.

Verse 7 carries a curious and somewhat disturbing notion, however. I wonder what you make of it: 'But grace was given to each of us according to the measure of Christ's gift.' It looks as though there is inequality in the body of Christ. But surely we are all given the grace of Christ in equal measure! Well, remember that Paul is about to move into a paragraph on service, so he is preparing the ground. I think he is making two important statements. First, that grace is given in definite measure, so that Christians are not all absolutely alike in gifts and functions – though all Christians have Christ's grace. Second, that these differences are determined by the ministries we perform in the body of Christ. Grace is still grace and not merit! It does not come because of what we are or our personal abilities, but because of the sheer unmerited gift of our ascended Lord. I still believe that the best definition of grace is the one based on the letters: GRACE – God's Riches At Christ's Expense. Yes, made available through the cross and resurrection and given to us.

Forgive me for being personal, but I want to reflect for just a moment on what it has felt like being a bishop. My previous jobs – as an incumbent of a very busy church and then as Principal of one of the largest theological colleges – were both very frenetic. I was still not prepared in any way for the workload of a bishop. It became very obvious to me why there have been examples of bishops burying themselves in committees, losing their vision and even their health. The volume of work is at times beyond belief. How can you prepare properly when you have at least ten talks a week to deliver, people to counsel, meetings to go to, articles to write, committees you have to attend in London? I realized that it would be wrong to ask for a lesser load, but it was right to ask for grace to transcend the load. I have remarked to more than one person that my testimony is now to that remarkable grace of God which can take ordinary people to know the extra-ordinary power of God.

Just before Easter I took a confirmation service at King's Taunton. It was a very hot morning, and there were sixty-eight candidates. Things went wrong, and I was not happy with the atmosphere. The parents looked as lively as cod in a fishmonger's shop. It was awful. But during the reception a man came up to me with his granddaughter who had been confirmed, and he said: 'Bishop, this morning you brought me back home. The last time I was in church was years ago. But I found the service and your message so helpful that I made my communion and I decided to follow Christ again.' In reality the service *was* awful; it was bad – and yet God used it. That's the point about grace. It is God's, and he administers it sovereignly through weak people like you and me.

Verses 11-16 remind us of how we can be worthy ministers of Christ. What were and are his gifts? They are that some are appointed in the body to minister to it and for it and on its behalf. The list here is similar to other lists in the New Testament. I don't want to dwell on them except to remark that the ministries referred to describe what the Church should be: an apostolic Church, a prophetic Church, an evangelistic Church, a pastoral Church and a teaching Church. The fault of the Church has been that our doctrine of ministry has been too static; we have thought of it as a thing in itself instead of a gift in the body! But ministry is important, someone will cry! Of course it is important – but important for what? We are told for what – to equip the saints for the work of ministry. To get them going.

The word 'equip' is a wonderful word coming from the root to 'fit together' – as in surgery to convey the idea of setting a bone. But it was also used to describe the function of mending nets. Isn't that a fascinating description of an important function we have on behalf of the saints? The work of surgery – fitting together broken people in the body of Christ; the patient mending of a broken net of communications in the body of Christ. All this is for the function of the saints, being the Church in the world, and for building up the body of Christ. We sometimes hear the word 'enablers' used of the ordained ministry. Think very carefully before you limit the definition of that word. True, we are to facilitate and enable, but we are still apostles and prophets and teachers and pastors. There is a ministry to which we were called and are being called and will be called. You are what you are, before you do what you do.

What then is God's dream for his Church? It is to be truly his body. Consider Paul's glorious vision. How many of us hold out such a hope for our congregations, let alone for ourselves! 'Until we all attain to the unity of the faith and of the knowledge of the Son of God, to mature manhood, to the measure of the stature of the fullness of Christ.'

Do you see the progressive movement of Paul's thought? What a wonderful vision this really is! 'The glory of God', Irenaeus finely remarked in the second century, 'is man fully alive.' The negative side of this – verse 14 – is to be no longer children, tossed this way or that way with every wind of false doctrine. There is a tendency these days to belittle theological knowledge, depth in teaching, hard thinking, troublous questions. I beg you, do not think that maturity in Christ means rejection of thought and hard theological slog. Our theology, our thinking, must be our gift to the body of Christ and we must make sure that we hone our faith to make it intelligible and accessible to those within and without the Christian family.

Paul's wonderful theology – because that is what it is – ends with a soaring conclusion in verses 15-16, back with the Lord again, in asserting the unity of the body of which we are members, joined and knit together.

What a curious business it all is, when all is said and done. When we look at the Church we can see so very clearly its imperfection and warts, but God sees the glory of the people of his Christ and he is hopeful. There is a marvellous passage in C.S. Lewis's *Screwtape Letters* where the devil encourages Wormwood to dupe the Christian into believing the Church to be weak and divided. The devil warns: 'As long as he does not see it as we see it – as an army with banners.'

III. *The Message of the Church*

You may recall the opening sequence of the TV series 'Star Trek', as the vastness of the universe opens up before the tiny spaceship. Such is the awesomeness and greatness of God. Here in 2 Corinthians 5, Paul is working from the same theology of the largeness of God, and he puts before us an exciting challenge.

Paul has just said that everyone has to appear before the final tribunal of God. He says in verse 11: 'Knowing the fear of the Lord, we persuade men.' But what do we make of such antiquated notions such as 'fear' and 'judgement'? Well, for a start, don't be in too much of a hurry to dismiss them as antiquated. It is true that modern people are not exactly given to contemplating judgement, and in an important sense our attention should not be on such notions in the first place. Rather we should begin with the majesty, holiness and mystery of God. God who confronts us as that *Mysterium Tremendum*, Wholly Other. Sadly, because people have lost sight of that vision of God, they have lost a sense of holiness and their moral codes have become correspondingly bankrupt, because there is no ultimate court of appeal.

Now Paul, in this passage, was trying to work out two things. First, he was trying to defend his apostleship against those who questioned his orders. We might parody it in this way: 'He wasn't properly ordained, you know . . . never went to the right college . . . the wrong hands were laid on him . . .' Seriously, it is a terrible burden when you are trying to exercise a ministry which is rejected by those you are seeking to work with. Yet Paul was at the same time seeking to work out his theology of God's salvation and he sets it before us so splendidly.

But how do we preach and speak about the 'fear' of the Lord today? I suggest that you go about this very carefully, because we are *not* told that it is what we should do. Rather, because we know the fear of the great and wonderful God *we* persuade men and women. That is our first motive.

Our second motive, however, is far more important and is the context in which fear should be put. Verse 14: 'The love of Christ constrains us.' The verb there is stupendous: *sunekei*. It occurs in Luke 12.50 where our Lord says: 'I have a baptism to be baptized with; and how I am constrained until it is accomplished!' The verb means to be 'squeezed in between'; like a fast flowing river squeezed between the walls of a gorge. The Lord was squeezed in between his love for his Father and his love for us. We Christians are squeezed in between Christ's love for us and our concern for others. This is – or should be – the motivating force for our ministries. If it is not, make it a matter of daily prayer until you lose yourself in the love of Christ. You see, Paul is saying something like this: 'Since I met my Lord, the great and compelling force of my life is that love which comes from God and that love which I offer back. My ministry is dictated by that love.'

Then we say: How can I know that love and take it in? You can't know it; it can only be received. It reminds me of that lovely saying of Mother Julian: 'By love he may be grasped, but by thinking never!' The theologians among us understand and wince a little!

Look how Paul continues, in verses 14-15. Here we enter the deep waters of theological controversy which I must now navigate carefully. Here before us swirl all the currents of controversies about substitutionary theories, representation theories, exemplary theories, and so on. I hope you understand me when I say that I am weary of all that. It is not because the theories aren't useful, nor because they don't matter, but because I feel that sometimes we are forcing our theories upon Holy Writ and making it into a kind of 'wax nose' for our pet ideas. What I think I am struggling to say is that you can't put the compelling love of God in a box or reduce God's mysterious work of redemption to a theory. Of

course, there is something wonderfully true about the substitutionary theory that God loved me and took my place; of
course, Forsyth's representative theory that Christ became on
the cross the representative figure of the human race merits
our attention. But in the end all these majestic ideas are but
the rough pencil drawings of an artist's first stab at a work of
creation. God loved me *so* radically, *so* staggeringly, that he
gave himself for me, for you, for us, for the human race. *For
all.*

If you are a Catholic by tradition, the sacraments will speak
to you daily of the Christ who gave himself on the cross for
you – *ephápax* (Hebrews 10.10). Once for all it happened and
therefore the sacrament is efficacious. If you are an Evangelical, of course you believe he died for you back there – *ephápax*
– but remember that his death is eternally valid and efficacious in the sacraments and in the other means of grace for
you and me. You see, this dying and living is both Catholic
and Evangelical.

Once, as I listened to David Jenkins, I had a wonderful
thought that I am going to patent. As he spoke of the wonder
of God I played around with the idea of 'one holy catholic and
apostolic Church' – and then I saw why we have such a
problem with these terms. It is because such terms belong first
of all to God. I believe in one holy catholic and apostolic God!
What a great idea – well, I think it is – a God who is one, holy,
apostolic, and catholic. And his love is like that too . . . ever
reaching forward to take us all in!

What a radical love this is! Paul says that at the heart of this
fascinating universe there is personal love. Yes, a God so great
that this amazing universe cannot contain him, yet so intimate
that the human heart can know him. This is our God.

Let us look now at the love which renews. Verse 17 goes to
the very heart of the Christian message: 'If any one is in Christ,
he is a new creation.' *En Christo.* In Christ, which is to say, my
spiritual and your spiritual address; our location, where we
are at home.

Now be very careful how you interpret the rest of the verse:
'the old has passed away, behold, the new has come.' Christians have shut up shop and waited for heaven to arrive,
treating this life as but an ante-room of heaven, denying their
emotions and bodies and societies. No! What we must hold in

tension are two important ideas. First, the old *has* gone. Yes, the aorist tense does indicate that the old way of living has been done away with. But, secondly, the new *has* come and the perfect tense is used to denote that there is continuity between old and new. The old way of living and old attitudes belong back there, but God the Creator ever creates, and *old things become and continue to be new*. Do you see what Paul is getting at? The newness of God's creation is not like the newness of our clothes which reach the point of shabbiness and have to be discarded, but the *newness is ever renewed*! 'New every morning is the love.'

Now I find that exciting. It means that nothing good is ever lost. God *recapitulates* every good thing . . . death is swallowed up in victory. Paul is so excited that he lets out an exclamation: 'behold'. Revelation 21.5 repeats it: 'Behold, I make all things new.' What a romantic, cosy theology. No, it is certainly not romantic, because the implications for us are demanding.

Before I move on to my next point let me ask you this question. How can we live this newness? How may our diocese and its structures be renewed? For example, what about Synod? It has come under a certain hammering – a little unjustified, I believe. We may not be able to do much about General Synod, but we can do something about our Diocesan Synod. I would love to see it becoming more a place where we pray together, where we hammer out our strategy, where we make plans and stretch the muscles of our faith. Our next Synod will include next year's quotas and we can predict some of the discussion. 'Behold, I make all things new. I am the faithful God; I can be trusted. I am the God of Abraham who goes before you. I will take you into deep waters, but you can hold my hand.'

My final point brings us to the implication of the themes we have been looking at. We have been given something: the ministry of reconciliation.

This is essentially what Anglican ministry is all about: a ministry of Word and Sacrament; the preached word and acted word; the preaching of justification by grace through faith and the sacrament of it. Paul gives us a word for our ministries: *ambassadors*.

Now we all know what an ambassador is. He or she represents his sovereign in a foreign land. He speaks the message of his sovereign, he conveys the authority of his sovereign and he represents the power of his sovereign. That, says Paul, means you and me. We have the message, we have been given authority, and God's power to proclaim the word of life has been given to us as well.

This is your ministry and mine, not to be despised or abused, but desired and used. But, equally, we cannot simply assume that we can do the work of reconciling in the way that former generations once did. A few months ago I saw a cartoon which showed a monkey looking totally baffled, scratching his head. The caption beneath read: 'Just when I thought I knew all the answers, they changed the questions!' At times we may feel like that. But the task of interpretation has to go on. Bridges have to be built into the conceptual landscapes of our culture. We are called to use our creativity, to use skills of music, art, poetry and drama for the gospel of God, to bring Christ near to people.

If you have been to St George's Chapel, Windsor, you will be aware that in that chapel, in order for visitors to see the exquisite ceiling, mirrors on wheels have been made available so you do not have to use binoculars or strain your neck. You look down into the mirror and the glory of the ceiling above is brought near. Similarly, through the incarnation of Jesus, we see the Father because Jesus is the image of God. You and I have a small part in this wonderful task of making Christ known, because to us has been given the ministry of reconciliation.

21

The Renewal of the Episcopate
To the Anglican Evangelical Alliance, 1990

Some years ago I was asked to lead an ordination retreat for the Oxford diocese and to preach the ordination sermon. I did so and took the theme of servanthood as the core element in ministry. I remarked to the ordaining bishop over lunch that the incongruous feature of the service, which greatly disturbed me, was the apparent discrepancy between my address which enlarged on the theme of humility, lowliness and incarnation of Christian ministry, and that of the actual service which smacked of the very opposite – the serried ranks of laity, readers, junior clerics, canons of the cathedral with the bishop bringing up the rear resplendent in his cope, mitre and pastoral staff. 'What tale of ministry were we really telling?' I found myself asking. What type of ministry were we saying was really important?

We could so easily forget that we are essentially talking about one single ministry which is the apostolic role of preaching and teaching Christ. Everything we do in church life is a devolution of that. The key verse is Mark 3.14: 'And he appointed twelve, to be with him, and to be sent out to preach.' This at heart is the ministry of those who follow the Servant – to be with him and to be sent from him to tell others. That is the sacred task of all followers and is central to all ministry. Let us never forget it.

We must also never forget that no validation of, or pattern for, monarchical episcopacy, as we know it, can be read directly from the New Testament writings. To suggest otherwise is to ignore the library of scholarship which has been produced over the last hundred years on this theme. The claim, sometimes made by Evangelicals, usually of the house-church variety, that there is a simple New Testament ecclesiology, or the opposite claim by other groups that the New Testament and the Early Fathers provide irrefutable support for their own type of episcopal government, is denied overwhelmingly by scholars of all Churches. 'All have won and all shall have prizes' was B.H. Streeter's famous egalitarian sentiment.

This is not to say that church order is unimportant. Principles on which oversight and pastoral care should operate can be drawn from the Scriptures, especially from the ministry of the Lord and the words and actions of the apostolic circle. We are right in emphasizing that, strictly speaking, the apostles have no successors – their authority now resides in their writings – but there is a basis for asserting that those who succeed the apostles in oversight are to serve as a focus of unity for the Church catholic. In emphasizing the Evangelical truths of apostolic teaching, Evangelicals must not ignore the necessity not only to keep and guard the faith – but also to pass it on (*traditio*).

As far as I am aware the Early Fathers did not deny either of these themes. We find a great concern for apostolic truth in writers such as Ignatius, Irenaeus, Cyprian and others, and the bishops' role as carriers of apostolic tradition. Together with this we see an awareness of the bishop as leader of the community as *episkopos*. Indeed, as Edward Schillebeeckx shows, the Church of the first three centuries continued the New Testament thrust that ministry is necessary for building up the Church along apostolic lines. Insofar as it does not do that, it is unapostolic. Episcopal ministry, in all its forms, is thus a service to the apostolicity of the Church.

Now, time does not allow me to show the inevitable developments in the early period but it is with that brief introduction that I want to go on to offer some reflections on the Anglican theology of episcopacy.

It is the claim of Anglicans that our faith is both Catholic and Reformed. At the heart of this is the distinction drawn by the Reformers between the inward essence of the Church and external polity which is the structure of ecclesial life. Putting it a little sharper, ecclesiastical polity belongs to the external form of the Church (*externa forma ecclesiae*) whereas the gospel is of its essence. Although the English Reformers avoided Luther's conclusion that the threefold ministry of bishops, priests and deacons was a purely human arrangement, our

Reformers agreed that the polity of the Church belonged to the sphere of *adiaphora*, things indifferent; things indifferent, that is, as concerns our salvation. Hooker, the greatest Anglican theologian of the Reformation period, accepted this, although he also asserted that episcopacy is of divine origin because such an ancient foundation must have had the blessing of God. Hooker, however, preferred the word 'accessory' to 'indifferent' because he believed the word accurately depicted the role of the ministry as accessory to the Word and the Sacraments in enshrining, applying, protecting and hallowing them.

Because the monarchical episcopate was considered to be a cherished and indispensable element in the structure of the Church, the Reformers resisted the radical call of Anabaptists and others to root out the traditions of men and return to the simplicity of the New Testament practice. Jewel, Hooker and Field knew that this was impossible anyway, but they also believed that the structure itself was reformable, not wrong. Thus, as we know, the ordination rites were not drastically altered but rather adjusted to bring them into line with Scripture and the traditions of the Early Church.

Interestingly, there was one very striking omission that I regard as regrettable. In the First Prayer Book of Edward VI, at the consecration of a bishop the Archbishop laid the Bible upon the neck of the newly ordained bishop with the words: 'Give heed unto reading, exhortation and doctrine . . .' Here was a sign of obedience, going back to Hippolytus' *Constitutions*, to an emphasis on apostolic doctrine and teaching. The charge to the newly ordained man was that he and his ministry should be subservient to the authority of the apostolic word. What a pity that this glorious symbol of ministry was lost! What was not lost, however, was the strong conviction that the Anglican doctrine of episcopacy was a valued tradition that belonged to the ancient Church and was a gift of God to his people. This, I suggest, is something for Evangelicals to heed, that Anglican ecclesiology assumes that the Reformation made no new Church. Hooker rejected the charge made by Roman Catholics that this Church was novel. He wrote:

As if we were of the opinion that Luther did erect a new church of Christ. No, the church of Christ which was

from the beginning is and continueth unto the end . . . We
hope therefore that to reform ourselves if at any time we
have done amiss is not to sever ourselves from the church
we were of before. In the church we were, and we are still.
(*Laws of Ecclesiastical Polity*, I.)

For Hooker, the Anglican Church is the Catholic Church of
Christ which washed its face through the painful process of
reformation. Customs and ceremonies that we have retained,
claimed our Reformers, are not the property of the Church of
Rome or any Church, but have been handed down by our
'Fathers'.

Integral to the nature of Anglican ecclesiology is that of a
fellowship of churches (diocese) in communion with their
bishop. Beyond that, is a fellowship of dioceses bound with
one another in a common and agreed structure of theology
and discipline. Such a description rules out congregationalism
on the one hand and papalism on the other. The participation
of bishops, priests and people in the government of the
Church eventually led to the crystallization of the principle of
two balancing authorities; that of the bishop on the one hand
and the 'bishop in council' on the other. In other words, an
Anglican church is episcopally led and synodically governed.
This may get a hollow laugh from anyone knowledgeable with
General Synod and it may get an even hollower laugh from
bishops who may feel infuriated with the goings-on of
General Synod, but the principle is clear, even if the practice
is imperfect.

This, in summary, sets out the theory of episcopacy we have
received, but the reality of it in our day and age may suggest
that there is an urgent need for a reformation of structure. Let
me urge a word of caution. As a new bishop I want to speak
as someone who does not believe that the present system we
have received is unworkable. We must not 'rubbish' what we
have received but find ways to renew and re-form our structure and, in this particular case, the episcopal office.

Why is this necessary? What has essentially changed is not
the character of our ministry in its threefold form, but the
nature of the country we serve. We are no longer living in a
society which we all may safely assume to be a Christian land.
We are living in a secular society with fragile links with the

Christian faith which once nourished its laws, customs and morals. Our context, therefore, is most emphatically mission-ary and the role of ministry has shifted from pastoral minis-trations to outreach and mission. I remember Archbishop Blanch telling ACCM Selectors some years back: 'We are no longer looking for pastors but for men who can lead the mission of the people of God.' I hope that the ACCM Selectors paid heed to that stirring call, but I would say that this is also relevant for those called to the episcopate. This takes me into the main thrust of my address, and to my submission that the renewal of leadership must take seriously the following framework for episcopal ministry.

The bishop-in-mission. My experience of the episcopate so far is that the bishop's office is almost totally conditioned by past practices. We have received a form of ministry which is domi-nated by pastoral and parochial modes of working. Episcopal ministry is largely reactive. We respond to what the diocese needs and wants, we respond to what our Archbishops and Standing Committee of the House of Bishops require, we respond to what the Synod with the bishop requires of us. Of course, there is room for initiative and we all stamp our own character and personality on the way we do things. But I don't think it is possible to contradict the fact that the role of a diocesan bishop is largely a responsive ministry. To use an analogy from football, the bishop is more of a sweeper than a striker. It is not for him to launch an attack on goal; received lore dictates that he handles the problems that get past others. He is there to defend and control the game from the rear.

As the thrust of this conference is intended to be practical as well as intellectual, let me tell you of my practice. From the start, I made it my intention to be a 'bishop-in-mission', which for me takes the form of going into parishes or deaneries five or so times each year from a Wednesday to the following Sunday. I go with a team of lay people, and with other support staff, to encourage faith, to share faith and to teach the faith. So far I have conducted seven or eight missions of this type and there is great enthusiasm for it. Why? It is because people are delighted that the bishop cares enough for them to spend that degree of time with them; because they are thrilled when the bishop spearheads mission and is seen to be leading it; because the clergy and lay leaders, who are exercising their own *episkopé*, are enormously cheered when their bishop is articulating his faith alongside theirs and offering stimulus and support. As the bishop in question, it inspires me as I see God working in the lives of people. Finally, and most significantly, it gives my episcopal ministry its rightful context. To go back to my footballing analogy, the bishop has become a 'striker'.

Our Church is beginning to set goals for the Decade of Evangelism. If this is to be taken seriously we must encourage the bishop to be a leader who 'leads the mission of the people of God'. Churchmanship is not an issue. Evangelicalism is not the *sine qua non* of a bishop-in-mission; what is essential is that the leader must be a person of faith, who loves Christ and wants to make him known – because *true episcopacy is rooted in apostolicity* and the bishop must be set free to lead mission. The sweeper must be allowed to change positions and lead the attack; who knows, he might even start scoring goals!

There is a second element which overlaps quite considerably with the bishop-in-mission and it is *the bishop as a teacher*. This, the early Church considered to be a fundamental ministry of the bishop; the teaching office was central to his task and the cathedral was his *cathedra*. In my reading of the lives of the great bishops of the second to fifth centuries, I note many examples of bishops who spent a large proportion of their time teaching the faith. There were bishops like Ambrose whose teaching took the form of apologetic preaching. Some of his preaching was 'pre-evangelistic' in that he explored theological opposition to the Christian faith and showed its inadequacy. At other times he taught the Scriptures, teaching the faith clearly, painstakingly and well. There were teachers like Augustine who used his *cathedra* to develop doctrine – hammering out his theology in public before committing it to writing. For these and many other teaching bishops, the faith was important to them; they believed it passionately and it showed in their lives and flowed from their lips and their pens.

What does this have to say to our situation today? I believe that our urgent task is for the Church to seek out people who are teachers of faith and who can lead the process of education within the community of the Church and argue for the faith outside the Christian body. This must not be construed by

Evangelicals as bishops whose main gift is expository preaching; that is not a wide enough description of the ministry of the teacher. It will require us knowing our world and culture, and responding to the challenge of our society to present an intelligent faith that will meet the minds as well as the hearts of intelligent people. But as I see it, this can only be done if the bishop is rooted in the faith of the Church and in its traditions.

Not far behind these two priorities I put the task of *the bishop as a leader of the community*. Whenever I institute a minister I never fail to be struck by the charge, 'Receive this charge which is both yours and mine.' If it is mine as well as his, what degree of accountability is built into our present system? Well, to be frank, very little. The freehold makes it possible for an idle priest, a visionless priest, and even an incompetent priest to disregard his bishop. The majority of our clergy are nothing like that, of course; a great deal of conscientious and wonderful work goes on in many of our parishes, but this is often in spite of bishops, not because of them.

It was A.J. Balfour who remarked to Hensley Henson: 'It seems to me that the bishops have no power to make clergy do their duty but just enough to deprive them of their rights!' However, it is frustrating for bishops who want to see growth that a 'hands-on policy' is made difficult by our structures. This, of course, would mystify and shock professionals in other walks of life whose ideology and long-term goals fall far short of ours. Somehow, the bishop has to take back the initiative, to be leader of the community, to be in a position to influence goal setting and to deploy people so that real needs can be met and churches built up. Now, to be sure, most bishops are doing their best within the limitations of the episcopal system we have, but more can and should be done. Personally, I am convinced that the freehold of all clergy, including bishops, should be terminated so that true accountability can follow and in reality therefore the parish may be the bishop's 'cure' as well as the incumbent's.

My last element is the traditional one, *the bishop as a pastor*. I have no intention of demoting the pastoral; indeed, it is important to me – I try to be a good pastor. Our ministry as pastors undergirds the leadership we wish to exercise. The personal support, inspiration and affirmation the bishop is able to give must, of course, be an important element in the episcopal office, but we should not exaggerate it out of all proportion to the other elements I have mentioned. Bishops share that episcopal ministry with archdeacons, Rural Deans and fellow ministers – let alone very able lay leaders who also very properly tend the flock of Christ.

Now the big problem is: How on earth can a bishop find time to be a 'bishop-in-mission', a bishop in teaching, in leadership and in pastoral care? The plain fact is that he (and the time will come when we will say 'she'), cannot be as single-minded as that unless there is a ruthless pruning of other things so as to allow him to be that kind of bishop.

Let me offer some suggestions.

First, if bishops are overloaded and dioceses are over-large, the Church should be addressing this serious managerial problem. No commercial enterprise would tolerate a system where efficiency and growth was held back by over-large departments. They would find ways of multiplying units so that the needs are addressed. It is a fact that the Church has not lacked the imagination or the muscle to do exactly that! My diocese was carved out of the diocese of Sherborne in AD 909 and it was clear then that the area was impossibly large for the then bishop to exercise a realistic ministry. Where there is a will, there is a way. But if that suggestion is not greeted with favour, then the reasonable acceleration of growth in auxiliary bishops, area bishops and suffragan bishops should be contemplated.

However, it has to be said that I do not notice a great deal of enthusiasm for this suggestion in the Church, so perhaps we could consider the second suggestion: the sharing of epi-scopal ministry. Let us go back to my earliest remark in which I insisted that all ministry essentially goes back to the one single apostolic role of preaching and teaching Christ. This suggests that episcopal ministry is essentially a shared one. The Anglican model of ministry is that of all ministry flowing from the bishop's office – thus the logic is the devolution of non-essential 'episcopal' functions to others. Why should he have to chair all those meetings? Why does he have to attend them? Why does he have to answer all those letters? Our natural instinct, because of our sensitivity to people, is to answer every letter we receive – but you will not find a Minister of the Crown being so concerned. She or he has already worked out her priorities. We could go on. What about those confirmations which take up so much time? Surely there are ways in which bishops should dictate the policy and not yield to 'it has always been done this way, Bishop'.

Finally, what about the neglected middle management of the Church, the faithful Rural Deans whose recognition is long overdue? I am convinced myself that it is this element of episcopacy which is the Church's greatest weakness. Is there not a case for the upgrading of the role of Rural Dean so that this becomes a permanent position and is paid accordingly? I think the case for this is very strong and I hope that our Church might work towards the strengthening of the middle-tier episcopal ministry of our Church.

Rereading this paper makes me wonder if I have been over-critical of the present experience of the episcopal office. Perhaps. I certainly do not want to belittle the splendid and sacrificial ministry being done by our bishops, and I acknowledge that my brief two and a half years hardly give me any authority to pontificate. Furthermore, I am only too well aware of the power and grace of God to transcend our failure and weakness, whatever the ministry and office we exercise in the name of the Lord. I never cease to marvel at what he accomplishes in spite of us and our structures. Nevertheless, if, as I said at the beginning, all ministry is a service to the apostolicity of the Church, or, as Hooker said, is 'accessory' to Word and Sacrament, then it is vital we should give attention to the episcopal office which is so central to the life of our Church.

I began with an illustration of an ordination service in Christ Church, Oxford, and the two messages sent out that day. I want to end with the challenge that particular story tells and which has been worked out theologically and practically in this paper. The root issue is this: What kind of episcopal ministry does the Church need today? What elements do we consider to be essential to its nature? It is the carefully considered and constructive response to that question which could help to influence the nature of leadership within our Church and shape the whole ministry of the Church. The only authority that ultimately matters is God's and his concern is that the Church should so proclaim the unsearchable riches of Christ that all may be brought to own him as Lord.

22

God's Power to God's People
Two talks given to Hereford Clergy, May 1990

I. God's Power Through Weak People

In both of these talks I want to share some thoughts with you as to how we may become more positive, dynamic people working for and with God, and how the structures of your diocese and your parishes may be more open to God the Holy Spirit.

First, then, 'God's power through weak people'.

The New Testament puts forward two almost contradictory pictures of power. First, there is the power of Jesus and the apostles and the apostolic Church in healing, saving and renewing. This power is dynamic and transforming. Consider Jesus saying to the leper, 'You are cleansed'; to the blind man, 'You can now see'. Consider the scandal, at least that is how I feel it, when Jesus in John 14.12 says: 'He who believes in me will also do the works that I do; and greater works than these will he do, because I go to the Father.' Well, the early Church certainly seemed to do these greater works. What about us?

Look a little more closely, and a different picture emerges. This powerful, charismatic Jesus is tired, at times angry, at times apparently distressed, and weeps at death, at the defiance of Jerusalem in rejecting him: 'Oh, Jerusalem, Jerusalem . . . How often would I have gathered your children together as a hen gathers her brood under her wings, and you would not!' (Matthew 23.37). Now we see a Church which does not seem to be as powerful as we first thought, but rather persecuted and its members fleeing in terror and dying. We see in it apostles such as Paul revealing acute signs of depression. For example, in Philippians 4.13, we see Paul in prison remarking: 'I can do all things in him who strengthens me', but the 'all things' apparently does not include getting out of prison!

Now, are these contradictions or integral parts of the mystery and magic of the Christian life? Well, let us see what happens if you ignore either of the elements. If you totally concentrate on the 'power' model, a distorted view of ministry and the Church emerges. It will become triumphalistic; it will not accept such an intolerable interference as unanswered prayer or an unhealed or powerless Christian. It will sweep under the carpet any notion of helplessness, or even doubt. It may end up with a 'prosperity' gospel because, after all, we follow a Christ who has given us the victory. I can promise you that what will result is what I call 'holy history': the gulf between what happened back there and my present experience which I am expected to deny.

Yet, equally, if we concentrate totally on weakness and wallow in it and say: 'God has called me to be a failure, I mustn't expect prayers to be answered, people to be won for God, churches to be filled to capacity', we end up making a virtue out of un-success.

What I hope you will see running through my two addresses is the bringing together of these two themes: power and powerlessness, strength and weakness, divinity and humanity, as inseparable elements in the life of God, in the life of the Church, and in the life of each of us.

In the biography of Max Warren, *Crowded Canvas*, the moving tale is told of him going as a young missionary to Nigeria. Everything seemed in his favour: he was very bright, very able and very ambitious to succeed for God. Yet within six months he was back home, his health shattered, his faith in God badly knocked, and clinically depressed. He went to a convalescent home and there met an older man who helped him back to faith. Warren one day said bitterly: 'Oh, how dark it all is. I feel I am at the bottom of a well and there is no one there.' The older man said gently: 'My dear Max, let me tell you something. The word "adventure" comes from a root meaning to come up against real trial. You will get through it, and I have to say that you have not yet reached the bottom of your well. But when you do you will not be alone, there will be someone there, and his name is Love.' Warren relates that that conversation was to be the turning point in his faith and life, separating an adolescent Christianity from a mature faith.

What about you and me? This conference gives us a wonderful opportunity to evaluate our ministries, noting those points of weakness and strength. How long have we been ordained? Five, ten, fifteen, twenty, thirty or maybe even forty years or more. What do we have to show for it? Not a lot, we might be honest enough to admit. And it is difficult to assess success in ministry. We spend a great deal of our time preaching, teaching, cajoling, administrating, bullying, writing, and sitting on the numerous committees we are to attend and service.

Let me say frankly, as a comparatively new bishop, that the majority of clergy get on with their work tirelessly, sacrificially and heroically. However, there are always the few who lose their way; their vision is blurred, their commitment is blunted, their prayer life shot to pieces and they are desperately hanging on. A minority drift into flirtation with the bottle and will not admit to themselves let alone the bishop, who can see it all too clearly, that there is a drink problem. Some drift into actual extra-marital affairs. Drink, sex, self-indulgence – yes, it is all too easy to do and none of us is in a position to sit in judgement because 'weakness' is our common name.

My own story as bishop is one of weakness and yet finding God's surprising power in it. The workload placed on bishops is quite phenomenal; it would not be tolerated in any other profession. Yet in spite of that load I have experienced the resources of God's grace to a remarkable degree. I hope that when the new Bishop of Hereford is appointed you will bear this in mind, and will be aware that he and his family will not only need to adjust to the pattern of strange life but that he has to get on top of the fast-moving life of a diocese and all the responsibilities that will come his way.

There is a second factor, no less important, and that is the renewal of faith. One of the great acids of Christianity is that of cynicism. We've all met it in our churches and we know of its destructive strength. We know of congregations where any enthusiastic idea is greeted with as much response as a dead cod in a fishmonger's window. The acid of cynicism is not reserved for Synods or PCCs, either, it is there when clergy come together and is expressed even when talk of God, prayer and Bible study is mentioned. As far as I know it could be here in this conference too. The kind of thing I have in mind is the reaction: 'Well, we've seen it all before . . . so what?' The reason why I can be confident that cynicism is around is because there have been many times when I feel it in myself and I have to bring myself to order and remind myself that I am under obedience to Christ.

Now, what is the reason for it and what is the antidote to it? The reason for it may very well be the point I made at the very beginning: the tension we must hold between God's power to do things and our weakness. We hear stories of success and we become cynical: 'Well, of course, he would say that, wouldn't he?' and so on.

The antidote may well be to consider our personal faith, and by this I mean our intellectual and conceptual faith. If your journey has been anything like mine, and I am sure there will be similarities, there have been times when our intellectual grasp of faith has not been brought into harmony with our spiritual journey. We may have entered theological training with great idealism and little knowledge of theology. There, at college, the acids of modernity were sown. Instead of theology becoming naturally part and parcel of our spirituality, theology is often treated as something quite distinct. The Bible becomes an object to be studied and theology a subject to be passed. However, we enter the ministry still full of idealism. Then we meet the average Anglican congregation which soon impresses us with its mature grasp of apathy, and the struggle of ministry begins to take its toll of our expectation and hope. We start to question God, our faith, our ministries. We might feel ashamed of this happening and push it away from us, disowning the questions while struggling on. That is not the way to handle it. We need to take on board that we are growing, travelling Christians. We don't know all the answers, not even the youngest person present, and we need always to ensure that our faith is in touch with and fed by our knowledge. In T.S. Eliot's 'East Coker' there are these splendid lines:

There is it seems to us
At best only a limited value
In the knowledge derived from experience.
The knowledge imposes a pattern, and falsifies,
For the pattern is new in every moment
And every moment is a new and shocking
Valuation of all we have been.

I think he is making the point that any system runs the risk of falsification because the pattern imposed limits the endless opportunity of fresh discovery.

You may know of A.J. Balfour's lines:

Our highest truths are but half-truths.
Think not to settle down for ever in any truth.
Make use of it as a tent in which to pass a summer's
    night,
But build no house in it, or it will be your tomb.
When you first have an inkling of its insufficiency
And begin to decry a dim counter-truth coming up
    beyond
Then weep not, but give thanks:
It is the Lord's voice whispering: 'Take up thy bed
    and walk.'

Now, you might think that I am advocating a dangerous form of liberalism; an uncertainty about Christian truth. Not at all! I am saying that sometimes unthought-out 'acids' rob us of a genuine trust in God and his power, because knowledge and faith are not meeting. A renewal of church life is impossible without the renewal of faith, and that is impossible without the renewal of our mind.

I find it sad when clergy are no longer reading widely around their special subject of God. We give feeble excuses: 'No time, sorry, Bishop. Would love to read more but there it is.' I actually do not accept this as a valid reason. We can all find time for things we regard as important. Perhaps we need to emulate the late Archbishop Ramsey when he was asked his practice about reading. He replied with a twinkle in his eye: 'I approach reading as an alcoholic approaches drink – a little but often.' This reaching forward to know our faith better must be rooted in the Trinity. This is truly to turn to basics; a God who loves the world and is committed to it – but his concern is for the coming of his Kingdom. Woe betide us if we replace his concern with our narrow obsession with the Church.

As we move into the 1990s, which we are calling the Decade of Evangelism, we must bear in mind that if we follow our Lord's command and commission and, indeed, his example, then evangelism will be rooted in the wholeness that God desires for all his creation. Let us beware of evangelism which stops with the individual. Important as it is for individuals to find personal faith and hope, that aim cannot be separated from our concern for them with one another in society, and, for that matter, the well-being of our environment. Salvation, community and ecology are not therefore three separate concerns, but overlapping areas of God's mission.

The work of the Father, of course, leads into the work of the Son, and this surely takes us into the area of what ministry is all about. Our task is to make Christ known. We often hear these days that this is the prerogative of the Evangelical movement. Let me scotch that myth. Some of the best evangelists have been Catholics; indeed, the Anglo-Catholic movement has spawned some remarkable missionaries, such as Bishop Frank Weston of Zanzibar. In the last century Father Aderley criticized a sermon by the nonconformist R.J. Campbell saying: 'It did not have enough gospel in it to save a tomtit!' Now, of course, I am not saying that our preaching and teaching have to be simplistic repetition of Sunday School teaching about Jesus as the way, truth and life. But I am saying that we have to find ways of communicating the Christian truth in fresh, intelligent ways that help to make the gospel 'tingle' for people. It is called 'good news'. Our problem is that it is not perceived as news at all. It is viewed as an old story about religious values, not as the breaking in of God's kingdom.

In William Abraham's book *The Logic of Evangelism*, he makes the point that to say 'God reigns' would not have been news for the orthodox Jew of Jesus' day. So when Jesus came and announced, 'The Kingdom of God is at hand', what did he mean? How was he understood? Abraham answers: 'The news is that God's reign now confronts the world directly and immediately in the person of Jesus and the call to 'repent' is to turn a complete U-turn and follow Christ.' In the 1990s, one of our key tasks must be to address this urgent question: How may the reign of God be perceived as good news today? How may we preach so that it becomes good news for others?

There are times when we doubt that it has the power to become good news again. But it can, and many of us have examples of people finding Christ and discovering the reality of that good news. Just a few weeks ago I took a confirmation service on Easter Eve. A couple was confirmed that evening with a few friends. The story behind their confirmation was that this unchurched couple had lost their only son in a tragic car crash. Through the ministry of the incumbent and a few Christian neighbours, the couple found support, meaning and hope, and made their journey through to a real faith and commitment. Even more remarkably, through this couple, some of their friends were confirmed as well. It was a very moving moment when I said on Easter Eve that: 'Through the gift of God's only Son, the loss of their only son is taken into the Father's heart and life begins from death.'

The gospel has to be preached to us so that it becomes fresh and wholesome once again.

Staying with the Trinity, however, must lead us to reflect on the nature and work of the Spirit as the pivot of renewal in our lives. The charismatic movement has emphasized greatly the work of the Spirit but, it has to be said, not always in a balanced way. To talk of the Spirit is to be aware of disturbing possibilities. I am afraid, however, that we have tended to domesticate the Holy Spirit with disastrous results for the Church. Many years ago Professor Raven said: 'If we are not quite in the position of the group that St Paul found at Ephesus who "had not so much as heard whether there be any Holy Ghost", at least there is amongst us grave uncertainty as to his Person and work.'

While the Renewal movement has reminded the Church of the significance of the Holy Spirit and, indeed, his Person and work – and for this, many of us are deeply grateful – there is the subtle temptation present in any group which is concerned with 'power', to treat it in terms of might, victory and success. I want to suggest again that the Spirit can become the *pivot* of renewal in our lives if we, for our part, can begin to accept that our weakness, vulnerability and spiritual poverty is the seed-bed of growth. It is in this unlikely context that God shows his remarkable ability to express his power through real people.

II. God's Power Through Weak Structures

The surprising and encouraging thing about God is that he does work through us – not in spite of us, as we often say, but because weakness is the clay that God uses to make his bricks. I caught a glimpse of this last December when I was addressing a large congregation in Wakefield Cathedral. There was a young man there who was deaf. He was signing for some other deaf people. I discovered to my astonishment that he was an organist and had been an organ scholar at Oxford University, even though he had been totally deaf from birth: an amazing sign of weakness triumphing over adversity. And that is the way of God. So Paul says in 1 Corinthians 1.27: 'God chose what is foolish in the world to shame the wise.'

How this challenges our attempts to gather power to us! Professor Rowan Williams remarked recently that Evangelicals, Catholics and liberals all shared this one conviction that while others in the Church had power, they as a group did not possess it! It should not worry us if we don't possess it, because power does have a way of corrupting people and institutions. I would like to encourage you to offer your insights and your church tradition to others as a gift. I came to faith through the Evangelical movement. I thank God for it, but over the years I have grown to love and appreciate other streams of God's life in the Church: the liberal, and the search for truth; the Catholic, and the reverence for tradition; the charismatic, and the openness to the Spirit. All these streams are given to the body of Christ and not to be despised. Yet none of these streams can claim to be the whole; they make distinctive contributions to the rich confluence of Christian truth.

Why is this important to recognize? Well, let us face up to the weakness of the Church in our land. Here is a sobering statistic: for the last forty years the churches of the UK have been steadily declining by 60,000 members a year. But, and here is an interesting statistic, the Church abroad has been growing by 80,000 new Christians a *day*! None of us can take refuge in a defence that we are doing very well. Even if we are, we must acknowledge that we are but scratching the surface. That is a strong argument for ecumenism – because we can no longer afford to do our mission and evangelism in isolation from each other. Thirty-seven percent of churches have less than twenty-five members!

There are no grounds for defeatism, however. Our cultured despisers seem to crow about the death of the Church of England; surely we should be very depressed about it all. No, not for a moment will I say that, because this is God's Church and not ours. Yes, the local church may die but the Church of Jesus Christ will root itself wherever there are men and women who are willing to confess him. We have seen amazing scenes of this over the last year or so. Last summer I was attending Conversations with Lutheran scholars and church leaders from the Nordic countries. We had a delegation from Latvia and Estonia. The Estonian people were deeply moved to be able to leave their country to meet other Christians; the last time they had had physical contact with other Christians was in 1938! They spoke of growth and hunger for God. The same goes for China and Russia. I read in the paper the other day about a programme for children's TV going out in Russia which in cartoon form is teaching the Bible!

Our question is, nonetheless: How may our structures and our life be more effective as channels of God's power and grace?

First, *we must look at our Church.* We are very fortunate to have the voice as the established Church. We have not always used this power and influence responsibly. I was reading a book the other day which showed the awful state of our Church two hundred years ago. In 1798 in St Paul's Cathedral the congregation numbered only six for the main service of Holy Communion. Six! The life of a prebendary of St Paul's was described as a 'life for a gentleman to do as little reading as he liked and dawdle as much as he wanted'! Today's Church is vastly different. We may be a less sleek animal but we have recovered our sense of mission in a way that was not true of the Church a hundred or even fifty years ago. I am proud of what we have done through the Church Urban Fund and through our leaders' involvement in political and social affairs. The press and TV are often asking me: 'Why are the bishops so political these days?' The answer is, of course, they are not political but they are more aware than ever of the political and social implications of the gospel.

Yet the ordinariness of the Church these days should not tempt us to think that power does not have its subtle place in our structures. Ambition and greed are there among us and we have to watch the demons in us and in our structures. Let me mention just two temptations that come our way.

There is, for example, the power to exclude others. I get very worried when I see signs of sectarianism in the Church. We might see it over rigorous baptismal policies. Yes, I under-stand the feeling that people should be able to say with a sincere heart that they 'turn to Christ', but who are we to drive people away? The Church of England does not minister only to its members but to all people in its society. Our Church is here not primarily to make pew fodder but to be salt and light in society and to lead people to faith. Incalculable damage can be done to the Church's mission when misguided priests have policies which drive people from well-intentioned and prob-ably naive folk religion into hostility to the Church and all that it stands for.

Another temptation is the other extreme, to deny doctrinal power. I want to remind you that there is a refreshing open-ness about Anglican ecclesiology. There is also a temptation to go to the other extreme and to be so weak and wishy-washy that we are seen as having no principles and no clear doc-trines. We have often been put into the shade by the Roman Catholic and nonconformist Churches, and we are beginning to rediscover that the 'power of the keys' is the proper exercise of the authority given to God's Church to exercise a ministry over and with people. This is also an element within Anglican ecclesiology: that with openness there comes commitment to the body of Christ.

Second, *we must begin to move from the mode of maintenance to mission.* Now I want to make it clear that I do not regard these as alternatives. I learnt a very important lesson when I was vicar of St Nicholas, Durham. I inherited a city-centre church which was shut six days a week, from Monday to Saturday, when thousands of people were around, and open one day a week when no one was around. It was my vow to open the church seven days a week to provide a Christian presence –

and it was a great joy to see that vision become a reality.

Maintaining beautiful churches must, of course, be our delight and joy. We should see our buildings as key resources for God. It would not be a good day for mission if we surrendered them to the State. Neither should our total concentration go on maintaining our buildings and structures. We must see them rather as a launch-pad for establishing God's Kingdom. I have to say with a little reluctance that I disagree with the Lambeth Resolution which suggests that evangelism is the main task of the Church. No, the life of the Church forms a threefold cord – mission, evangelism and worship. *Mission* takes in 'kingdom values' by way of responding to human needs and seeking to transform unjust structures. *Evangelism* is the task of leading people to God and helping them to accept Jesus Christ as Lord. *Worship* is the celebration of the life of the community around Word and Sacrament. These three must go together.

How may we respond to this challenge? This takes me to my third point: *we must mobilize the local church*. Why start with the local church? I'll tell you why; parish ministry is where the Church touches most people. The parish is the basic and essential unit of the diocese's life and mission. In the long run, if the Church fails in the parish, it fails. So how do we mobilize the local church to be more effective in its work and mission?

Let us first look at the pattern of the Lord. What did he do? Well, first we note the way that prayer was at the heart of his ministry and mission. We find him constantly in prayer, and that says a great deal about spirituality as central to the Church's life and work. Never think of prayer and mission as opposites; they are partners in the exciting work of bringing people to faith. Then notice from the Gospel record Jesus' way of bringing individuals to him for that life-changing encounter with the living God. We notice the way Christ brought together mission and spirituality: 'And he appointed twelve, to be with him, and to be sent out to preach' (Mark 3.14).

Then there was the mentoring that went on. He took these men with him; they saw him at work. Do we do that? I fear we don't, and our mission is the poorer for it. We see Jesus with a small group of people, nurturing them to follow him. I encourage you to work this out. I thank God for my first vicar who took that young fellow of seventeen and gave him books to read, scriptural texts to memorize, friends for fellowship. We so often drop youngsters in at the deep end. When I take confirmation services I often wonder what kind of post-confirmation nurturing will go on. If you are a musician and have a young musician who shows talent, you don't casually wave music under their nose and say: 'If you play this regularly, you will be as good as I am.' No, you will encourage them, play with them, take an interest in them, listen to their fumbling performances. Why aren't we mentoring people like that? We say: 'We haven't got time to do it.' The Lord did it, and we therefore have a christological example. Your best work is not necessarily with large groups of people but what you do regularly and often with the few whom you can influence for God.

Let me consider another point: mobilizing the local church must take the form of teaching the faith. How well does your congregation know its faith? I heard an international missiologist say some years ago: 'Anglicans are the worst taught of all Christian groups.' Now, I don't know how he found that out, but I don't wish to argue with it. I think he could be right. In Acts, the first community sat under apostolic teaching. We have that duty to teach and preach the faith. Is it being done with imagination, with sparkle and with joy?

There are, of course, many different levels to this, not only preaching from the pulpit but parish groups of all kinds. It is still not the case that every church has such groups. If you do, make sure that there is real input that will help the group to grow in its knowledge. I am also bold to say that it is still the case that our teaching is too middle class and intellectual. Simplicity must be the order of things, but not simplistic preaching. People will soon see through teaching which speaks down to them and they won't forgive that. They *will* appreciate teaching which addresses them as thinking people though not necessarily with oceans of theological knowledge.

Then what about worship and the life of the local church? Again in Acts we see the primitive Church in its worshipping life as it 'broke bread' together and shared its life. I have long been convinced that central to evangelism is pastoral care. Here in Acts the church of Jerusalem was doing that and things were happening as a result.

Do remember, however, the element of weakness as a

constituent part of the life of the Church. Bishop Geoffrey Paul once remarked shrewdly: 'There is no way of belonging to Christ, except by belonging gladly and irrevocably to the glorious rag-bag of saints and fatheads that make up the one, holy, catholic and apostolic Church'! I happen to believe that that is a profound understanding of ecclesiology. Weakness is the condition of the Church: saints and fatheads! If it is true, then it throws a great deal of light on what goes wrong in church life when the average congregation gets things out of balance.

There are times when I fully agree with Bishop Gore's remark about the Church of England, that it is 'a curiously devised instrument for the frustration of purposes it was designed to implement.' How *do* we help congregations to love and to be the kind of communities which start to look out in mission? There is no easy answer, but I do know this: that every situation is redeemable, every situation has some hope somewhere in the structures – all is not death and darkness.

What about worship? God's secret weapon for evangelism, someone called it. We might not think that about the average Evensong. But not so fast, I have evidence of very traditional services being effective tools for growth. For example, I had to preach recently at Matins and the order of service was the Book of Common Prayer. There was a very good congregation; we had warm, uplifting hymns; the readings were given extremely well; the service was well led. I could not fault it. It is patently *not* the case that a healthy dose of Alternative Service Book will bring them in their droves. It is the quality of what we do that counts, whether ASB or BCP, and I refuse these days to get caught up in that kind of antithesis. In my diocese the service that everyone is using with some success to bring newcomers is a very simple form of Family Service or Family Eucharist. We have all to find our own way, however, and not be legislated to by others.

Then there is the setting of goals and expectation of results. Do we ever set goals with our Parochial Church Councils? As long as they are not unrealistic, it can be very rewarding to reach for goals that at the moment are beyond us. For example, we see the Church in Acts expecting God to answer its prayers. Do we do so, bearing in mind what I have already said about watching the tension between power and weakness?

What kind of goals have I in mind? I remember years ago helping a church to decide its priorities. We met over a weekend and I asked them to write down what they regarded as long-term and short-term goals. The first session we ended up with forty different goals all jumbled up. The second session, we reduced them to five long-term goals and five short-term goals. There were still too many. In the third session, they were reduced still further to the following: *Worship:* to have a monthly Family Service; *Young people's group:* to start one; and (this is the one that excited me) to pray for ten per cent congregational growth. The church also had a long-term goal – to build a modest hall for the Sunday School and the wider community.

It thrilled the congregation when these goals were reached. The goals are all very obvious but not all that common in church life.

Then we see the Church in Acts meeting to pray as the Lord did throughout his ministry. We will get absolutely nowhere if prayer is not central to our life either.

My final point is that *we must mobilize the diocese and its structures.* If, as I believe, the structures of the Church have to reach outwards in service, so the structures of the diocese must reach out to serve the local churches. I have already said that the basic unit of the diocese is the parish, and if this is theologically correct (as I believe it is), then the centre of the diocese is not the Cathedral but wherever the parish is. This is what Dr Runcie meant by his remark some months ago that the centre of the Church lies in its circumference. It may not make sense in geometry but it is theologically sound! Do we believe that? Do our diocesan structures take it into account? I sometimes wonder. I get the distinct impression that the average congregation does not feel that it is the centre; there are times when it feels neglected and it has to scream in order to be heard. Here in vengeance is power and weakness. There is another matter, too: why is it that parish churches are expected to live by faith but dioceses never seem to do so? For example, it is rare to meet a synod which will say things about its financial policy and buildings that a PCC might say: We will trust God to meet our quota responsibilities. 'Trust God?' will question that florid colonel from Exmoor. 'That's a bit pious; we must see the colour of your money!' It is time that diocesan synods took more responsibility for strategy and for growth and this will mean Synod itself endeavouring to articulate its goals.

So let me conclude. Mission is not our work primarily but God's. We enter into his mission – and never let us forget it. His Church will not and cannot fail because it is locked into God's power and integrity. Our task is to offer him our weakness so that this frail channel may become his vehicle of grace.

23

Characteristics of a Growing Church

In May 1990 the Bishop did a visitation of the entire diocese.
He called clergy and churchwardens to see him and addressed
them in ten different centres. This was a typical address.

The main reason for this visitation is that, in response to the call to make the 1990s a Decade of Evangelism, this seemed an ideal time to meet with incumbents and churchwardens together and to share with you some ideas about growth – to share a vision for the diocese and our churches.

First, let us recall the situation we face in this country as far as faith is concerned. Whether we like it or not, the fact remains that we are a backwater of Christianity in world terms. We may pride ourselves on giving Christianity to the world through the missionary movement, but we are in reality but a shadow of the vigorous Church that God longs for us to be. A recent statistic given by the Bible Society reveals this bleakly enough: there are in the UK 43,000 churches of all denominations. Organized Christianity has been declining since the war by 60,000 members a year. Yet the worldwide picture is very different – there the Church is growing by 80,000 new Christians a *day*! Those churches that are growing would put us to shame by their life, their richness and their bold uncompromising faith. There is another statistic that I regard as significant: 37 per cent of all Protestant churches have less than twenty-five members. Thirty-seven per cent! That is a significant percentage. If we could find a way of giving a vision of growth to the small church – and indeed, to the larger church as well – we would find ourselves not in a death situation but in a life situation in which churches would once again find their mission and a reason for existence.

So, what are the characteristics of a growing church?

A growing church is prepared to face disturbing news

We are not always honest with ourselves, are we? I suppose this is typical of human nature. We have often heard Government spokespeople say about the economy: 'Yes, the inflation is bad, mortgage and interest rates are far too high, but the "upward trend" is good'! Sometimes I hear clergy say: 'We have good congregations – over a hundred usually.' But the reality may be very different; fifty or sixty on a good day. The wish, in such cases, is father to the thought. We'd love it to be a hundred regularly, but this is not the reality. There has to be, I want to submit, a realistic honesty about our ministries so that real growth can be prayed for and expected. To put it another way, there has to be a *holy* dissatisfaction with the work we are at present doing. We have to admit that however well we are doing in reaching people and getting them to church, we are all failures because we are only touching a minority of the population. So my first point to stress is *realism*. Are we really prepared to be honest before God and say: 'We have failed you and our ministries are hedged about by failure'? We often disguise the truth from ourselves, let alone God. Our mission begins with analysis of what we are doing and not with what we would like to do.

A growing church is concerned with God's mission and not its own existence

It is all too easy to confuse Christianity with the well-being of the Church. God is not concerned with the existence of the Church, as such. The Church must be an instrument of God's Kingdom; there lies God's concern, in building his Kingdom, and he will do it with or without you and me, with or without the Church of England. He can raise up other Christians to complete his work, if we fail or falter. Now this is an important point to hold on to because it is all too easy to concentrate on just what goes on in church or in the concerns of the Church. When we concentrate upon the Church the result is *consumerism*: concern with what we want; my worship; my way of running things; my building and so on. When we concentrate upon God's Kingdom we see life through kingdom values: we see the need to share the love of God with others; we see the poverty of others without the Christian message; we see young people with no strong moral world-view and we see the potential of the Church in addressing the issues all around us. Indeed the Archidiaconal Consultations revealed two other significant things: that many parishes are very concerned about their local communities and wish to take seriously their needs both with respect to outreach and in practical service. The other finding is that there is a concern that the diocese should think of the ministry of the Church in the world and, indeed, even environmental issues. It is my belief that if we are concerned with God's mission, you and I will never lose the note of excitement and the sense of adventure.

A growing church is concerned with the deepening of faith

I have a poster which shows a plant growing, and the words of John Henry Newman underneath declare: 'Where there is growth there is life.' A young plant is hungry to grow and a young Christian is hungry to learn. As a former theological college teacher, it was always a delight to have students who were hungry for knowledge; who slaved over their Greek; who were keen, yes, actually keen to know about Kant, Hume and Rahner! The students I worried most about were the ones who never asked questions, never seemed to explore the frontiers of their knowledge and did not seem to want to know.

Now, one very astonishing fact has emerged so far from the consultations with PCC groups. It is this: people are saying over and over again: 'We need to know our faith; we cannot share our faith at the moment because we do not have a sufficient grasp of it. We want to know Christ better.' This is almost tangibly coming through. How are we going to respond to this cry? Well, we must consider the ways that people learn and see if we can do things better than we are at the present moment. For example, are we making sufficient use of the opportunity of preaching in church? At the heart of preaching is teaching; are we teaching the faith? Those of us who are teachers of the faith, are we sitting under the Word and drinking it in and savouring its excitement? If we are not, how can we attract others to a drink which apparently does not satisfy our thirst? What about fellowship groups, Bible study groups, Sunday School groups? There is one common factor in all growing churches and it is this: they all believe in the importance of cell groups.

We are proposing in this diocese to set up a Bishop's Certi-
ficate for lay people, and this is one tangible way by which we
wish to respond to the cry that 'we need to know our faith'. I
hope that when this is launched in the next year or so, you
clergy and lay leaders will give this your support and encouragement. Quantitative and qualitative growth belong
together.

A growing church is concerned to harness the ministry of all its members

One of the great insights of our time is in fact a rediscovery of
the ministry of lay people. It is called in today's jargon 'every-
member ministry' and this means every person in church life
having a ministry to offer God. It may be as a Sunday School
teacher, as a sidesman, giving out books, or offering hospi-
tality. It may be offering something in the worship. Those of
you who heard the Chancellor of the diocese at Synod will
recall his exposition of the Canons which make it clear that lay
people can take services and be involved perhaps more than
they realize. This does not rule out the ordained ministry of
the clergy, but makes it clear that all of us in the body of Christ,
ordained and lay, have gifts to offer.

Now, this may find a response in two ways. First, a failure
on the part of some clergy to use lay people. This is as equally
true of Evangelicals as it is of Catholic clergy. Indeed, in a
well-ordered Catholic parish, the use of lay people in worship
is often quite imaginative and amazing! But sometimes it is
clergy who make it difficult for lay people to exercise a ministry. Why? Well, sometimes it is feared that the lay person
might do it better; sometimes it is because clergy have been let
down before and they feel that if they do it themselves, it will
at least be better done. We have to live with risk, I'm afraid,
and that, after all, is how people often grow! But another
response is the feeling that 'It is all very well to talk about lay
ministry but in my parish there are no lay people capable of
exercising any ministry at all', or: 'Our parish is not exactly
crawling with gifted people panting to be used in the ministry
of the church! Press-ganging is the order of the day!'

I do understand that; I am not implying that lay people are
standing around idle because the parish priest is hogging all
the ministry to himself. What I am saying is that we must find

ways to utilize the gifts of others if the mission of Christ is to be effective in our diocese and churches. It may be that clergy and others will have to acquire skills in delegation, or abilities in inviting others to share ministry with them. Again, may I say that this diocese has appointed a full-time officer to develop lay ministries and his services are available for us to use. If we don't utilize the strengths of lay people, the ministry of the Church will be impoverished in the days to come. What we have to take on board in this diocese is that ordained clergy are not going to become more plentiful. Indeed, we may have to face the bleak prospect of fewer clergy because of a drop in our Sheffield Quota. Let me add to this by saying again that many churches are using the gifts of lay people in all sorts of ways, and through them the life of the Church is being enriched. We owe a great deal to our lay readers, for example, who are making an effective contribution to the life of the diocese.

A growing church is concerned with quality of worship
Bishops and archdeacons spend a great deal of their time worshipping in many different types of churches in the diocese. It varies a great deal. Sometimes it can be High Mass, at another time a very low celebration of Holy Communion. It might be the Book of Common Prayer or it might be the Alternative Service Book; it might be a free form of Family Service. I do not want to make judgements on what we see going on. But I will tell you this: the quality of what is offered has a significant bearing on the growth of Christianity in that place.

Now what factors am I thinking of? Well, take the physical ambience of the building. Is it conducive to worship? If it is too cold it will affect people's ability to think, let alone worship. It is better then to worship in somebody's front room, than to endure minus ten degrees in a freezing church building! It may be the warmth of people welcoming others to worship, helping them to find their place in strange- looking books. It might also be the way the service is led that speaks of the holy, that makes it possible for others to pray. It might also be a service of endurable length to people. Why should we assume that God is twice as pleased with two hours of worship than half that length well led and well prepared? It might also be the way the place has been made beautiful for God with tasteful drapes, pictures, banners, furniture which help people to concentrate. It may also be the way the sermon is preached, the lessons read, the service sung that takes people out of themselves into the presence of God.

Worship is, of course, a most mysterious medium which defies our attempts to define it but I am convinced that it needs more attention, not less, by congregations if they are concerned to make it available to others. The lawyer F.E. Smith once remarked about Winston Churchill that 'Winston has devoted the best years of his life to preparing his impromptu speeches.' Well, I think that is often the way with worship. The better we prepare, the better we hone the human skills with devotion and love, the more it will come from the heart and be the unaffected and effortless gifts of human beings to a creator God. Worship, too, needs to be analysed.

Time does not allow me to spell out the challenge of developments beyond our diocese. We think of the enormous demands of the worldwide Church with all its needs. I'd like us to respond more effectively to the life of the Church beyond the diocese and I hope that as we travel through the decade our response may be more significant.

Meanwhile, there are three things we can do to make the 1990s an exciting place in the diocese. First, we need to analyse carefully, clinically and Christianly the actual work we are doing, and make an honest and objective evaluation of the life of our churches.

Second, our aims to make this decade a Decade of Evangelism will get absolutely nowhere if *prayer* is not the foundation stone of all we do. We see the Lord's pattern in praying for us throughout the years of his ministry. We can do no less. Could you consider your church finding new ways of getting people together to pray about the growth of the church?

Finally, we must expect great things to come from God's hand for us. We are engaged in *his* mission, not ours. He is responsible for results; at the end of the day we can only say: 'We are unprofitable servants – we only did what it was our duty to do.'

24

My Vision for the Year 2000
Presidential Address to Bath and Wells Diocesan Synod,
April 1989

We are entering the 1990s, and before we know where we are the year 2000 will be upon us. How do we prepare for it? What should we be doing? What priorities should we have in mind?

Now one thing we cannot do is nothing. You may have heard of the ninth Beatitude which goes: 'Blessed is he who expects nothing – he shall not be disappointed!' Neither can we wait for the inevitable – whatever that may be – to come upon us. Neither the ostrich with his head in the sands nor Rip van Winkle are patron saints of Bath and Wells! If you want a text there is an apt one waiting to be used in Proverbs 29.18: 'Where there is no vision, the people perish' as the Authorised Version has it.

Now vision is a most overdone word; what does it mean? Yes, we know it comes from the root 'to see'. But it means, in Christian thought, the capacity to enter into God's plans for his people; to think with the boldness and courage of the children of God; to dare to reach out and discover God's will. Claims like that, of course, are very risky. Who is prepared to say: 'I know what God wants for our diocese'? I do not make that claim. I make a more modest suggestion that we as leaders of the people of God in this place should start to make plans for growth. We should not take it as axiomatic that Christianity in this diocese should stagnate and die. Indeed not; I see every reason to reach out and discover a vision for our diocese. What kind of criteria should we have in mind? Let me put before you some suggestions.

First, I remain quite unrepentant that any talk of mission, evangelism and outreach must be rooted in *a deep spirituality*. Effective Christianity begins here in a sturdy acceptance of the

love of God, his presence with his people, and a rhythm of
worship, praise and learning that mark the people of God. In
our Anglican tradition we speak of the balance of Word and
Sacrament. Here in the worship of God we incarnate the reality of the Christian faith. Let us never talk of mission before
speaking of the reality of God among us. Mission never begins
because we need more people to fill our churches; what a
terrible motive for evangelism! No, mission springs from our
love of God and his love for us. Because he first loved us and
fills our lives with his grace we have something to share. So
the first thing we must attend to is the character of our worshipping lives: our walk with God; our desire to know him
and be known of him.

It is a thrill to me when I go into churches and find the place
well cared for – the notice board outside up to date, the church
clean and tidy and well decorated. It is an even greater joy
when I meet ordinary Christians with a faith that sparkles
with a love of God that even ecclesiastical duties cannot sup-
press! It is not surprising therefore that when one finds
growth in congregations, it often comes welling up out of the
devotion of the people. Faith springs from faith.

Out of that context arises the commitment of people who
want to give to others. Stewardship is not the giving of our
money to God. Why is it that when people hear the word
'stewardship' they shift uncomfortably and clutch their wal-
lets? Perhaps we should ban the word 'stewardship' and look
for other words to stand for our commitment to God's work.
Far more important than money is the giving of ourselves to
God. Often people in other walks of life and other voluntary
services are far more sacrificial in their offering of time than
we are, and we are put to shame by a commitment which
others make to their causes which staggers us. When churches
start to care about their work and desire to grow, and when
they decide that they will accept no longer the world's expectation that they should die, it is at that point that they start to
journey back to health again!

Second, to talk of vision involves us in *looking critically and
carefully at what we are like*, and even considering whether
growth is inhibited because of what we do or because of
attitudes which no longer cut ice today. For example, we will
need to study where the pockets of growth and decline are in

the diocese and ask: What are the factors that lead to growth, and what are those that seem to lead to decline? Factors that will come into our thinking will include population shifts, patterns of worship, styles of leadership, lay leadership, and so on. We will, of course, want to pay very careful attention to the Archbishop's Commission on Rural Ministry when it comes out.

Can I say here how much I appreciate and admire what so many of you are doing in small country parishes. It is a thrill to see the dedication and commitment of incumbents and lay people, and the way the Church is quietly and faithfully exercising a ministry at the centre of village life. It must never be thought that small numbers mean small and ineffective ministries. Indeed not. Often the ministry of the village is out of proportion to the actual numbers of people who are in church, and that is something we must never forget, otherwise we shall end up with a sectarian view of Church and society. Nevertheless, as we work towards a coherent plan for the diocese, it must begin from a realistic and even ruthless assessment of our strengths and weaknesses.

Third, I believe that our vision must involve *a strategy for ministry*. It is difficult to foresee what lies ahead as far as the ordained ministry is concerned. On the one hand we can see that in about 1993-4 we shall witness a great number of retirements from the ordained ministry in our diocese. On the other hand, the national figures do not give us great assurance that we shall be able to maintain our present numbers. You may already know that we have been asked to reduce our Sheffield Quota by six or seven priests.

Now this kind of situation gives us an opportunity to consider other ways of maintaining ministry and exercising mission. For example, a year or two ago I was talking with the Roman Catholic Archbishop of Bordeaux about the French problem where some priests have up to twenty-three churches to look after. I expressed my utter astonishment and must have said: 'How terrible!' He said: 'Not at all. What has come out of these situations has been exciting. New lay ministries have mushroomed and exciting family services. While we want more priests we are delighted that God has raised up new ministries.'

This reaction from a somewhat unlikely source encourages

us to take on board that our problems are often God's opportunities to break in with new directions and fresh ideas. I can
report that in a great many of our churches we are seeing the
involvement of many lay people in ministries, and we acknowledge that without them the work of God would collapse
overnight. The encouragement and stimulation of these ministries is very important, and I hope that we are doing that in
our different contexts. If I may trail a little of my thinking on
this issue, I would guess that we must start to consider very
seriously the possibility of local non-stipendiary ministry, and
see whether this is an option for our diocese.

Then, fourth, vision must include *evangelism and mission*. Of
late we have heard a lot about a Decade of Evangelism. Where
it came from is anybody's guess, although my money is on the
Pope who made mention last year of a decade of evangeliza-
tion for the Roman Catholic Church. Whatever its origin, at
Lambeth last year a motion was suddenly put forward calling
upon the Anglican Church to make the 1990s a Decade of
Evangelism. In one long sentence and in no more than forty
seconds the motion was overwhelmingly carried.

What did it mean then, and what does it mean now? Of
course we all agree that it would be very nice to have a Decade
of Evangelism. It is so far a costless statement. We could, for
example, easily decide this weekend that Bath and Wells
should ban all cars from our diocese, or that there will never
be a quota again, or that every parish should have its own
vicar. Reasonable sentiments, we may think, but when stated
out of context they have no cash value and are quickly forgotten. Will this be the fate of a Decade of Evangelism? Well, that
depends a great deal upon the way we set about dealing with
the questions and opportunities that present themselves before us. Indeed, I am happy to report that the BMU board and
the ACC of the Anglican Communion has established a working party called 'Mission Issues and Strategy Action Group'
(MISAG) who will be making practical suggestions for our
Communion.

Let me now mention a few of the issues that we must tackle.
First, what is evangelism anyway? What is the good news for
people who are indifferent to the Christian message? Does it
make sense and is it compelling? We cannot avoid the challenge of such questions. My job as bishop takes me to the

frontier of church life. I have wonderful opportunities of talking about the Christian Good News to people who are miles away from the Christian family and I know for a fact that there is a comprehension gap between them and us. There is a second question: How are we to reach people who feel no need of God? Yes, of course, we can invite them along to special meetings and to church meetings, but how many of them come? When they do come, how many of them find the message compelling? Finally, to what degree do we have to change ourselves in order to make the news good for them?

I hope you will not feel that in raising these questions I have any problems myself with the Good News! Of course not! For me Christianity is a coherent philosophy of life which has at its centre following a Person who makes all the difference to life. But we will need to work out what it is we are preaching, how we are doing it, and what we need to be and do in order to be more effective.

It comes down to this: 'If there is no vision, the people perish.' We face challenging times, but it is a good time to be alive and I am excited by the opportunities before us. Together under God we could see great things happening; divided we could see a great opportunity wasted. Let us work together to do God's work in God's strength.